THE
OLYMPICS

Facts, Figures & Fun

*"Any book without a mistake in it has had
too much money spent on it"*
Sir William Collins, publisher

THE
OLYMPICS

Facts, Figures & Fun

Liam McCann

ff&f

The Olympics
Facts, Figures & Fun

Published by
Facts, Figures & Fun, an imprint of
AAPPL Artists' and Photographers' Press Ltd.
10 Hillside, London SW19 4NH, UK
info@ffnf.co.uk www.ffnf.co.uk
info@aappl.com www.aappl.com

Sales and Distribution
UK and export: Turnaround Publisher Services Ltd.
orders@turnaround-uk.com
USA and Canada: Sterling Publishing Inc. sales@sterlingpub.com
Australia & New Zealand: Peribo Pty. peribomec@bigpond.com
South Africa: Trinity Books. trinity@iafrica.com

A catalogue record for this book is available from the
British Library.

ISBN 13: 9781904332404
ISBN 10: 1904332404

Design (contents and cover): Malcolm Couch
mal.couch@blueyonder.co.uk

Printed in China by Imago Publishing
info@imago.co.uk

For information about custom editions, special sales, premium
and corporate purchases, please contact ffnf Special Sales
+44 20 8971 2094 or info@ffnf.co.uk

CONTENTS

THE OLYMPIC GAMES

The Olympic Games is the greatest single sporting spectacle in the world. More than ten thousand athletes from over two hundred countries compete in thirty sports for that elusive gold medal, the pinnacle of any sporting career.

THE NAME

Historical records kept by the ancient Greeks tell us the first Games were dedicated to their Olympian Gods and held on the plains of Olympia in 776 BC, though it seems likely that an athletic competition had existed here for much longer. An Olympiad was the name given to the four year cycle between Games. The Games continued for more than a thousand years before the Christian Byzantine Emperor Theodosius banned all 'pagan cults' in 393 AD.

THE EARLY GAMES

The site of the first Games, Olympia, is in the western Peloponnese, in southern Greece.

Olympia was often used as a meeting place, as well as a place of worship for other religious practices. In its centre, the magnifi-

cent temple of Zeus dominated the temple of Hera. Inside the
main temple, Pheidas' spectacular 42-foot gold and ivory statue
of Zeus was one of the seven wonders of the ancient world.

According to Idaios Daktylos Herakles, Zeus defeated Kronus
in the struggle for the throne of the Gods and thus became the
Supreme Being. Herakles claimed Zeus had also helped him
conquer the Elis when he went to war with Augeas and so
staged the first Games in his honour.

The ancient stadium held more than 40,000 spectators. Special
outbuildings were used by the athletes to train in private while
many more housed the judges.

Young people were encouraged to participate to stimulate
competition between rival cities. Plato mentions how
competition improved their fighting ability at the *palaestra*
(wrestling school), which was a popular meeting place for
trainers and athletes.

Three kings signed the Olympic truce (*Ekecheiria*) – which
lasted a month – so that all people could travel to and return
from the Games in peace. Warring cities put aside their differ-
ences and assembled at Olympia to compete without violence.
The judges could banish entire cities if they broke the truce.
Athletes and spectators travelled from Greek colonies in
modern-day Spain, Libya, the Ukraine, Turkey, Egypt and those
bordering the Black Sea. The first athletes to arrive used the rest
of the month to train.

The ancient Olympics were classified into four eras. The
Archaic Era ran from 776-480 BC, the Classical Era from 480-

323 BC, the Hellenistic Era from 323-146 BC and the Roman Era from 146 BC-369 AD.

A flame was ignited by the sun (using mirrors) and kept burning for the duration of the Games, a practice that has survived today with the lighting of the Olympic Torch.

Champions received their awards at an official ceremony on the last day of the Games. A *Hellanodikis* (Greek judge) announced the winner by herald, then placed an olive tree wreath on his head and offered him a palm branch while spectators cheered and threw flowers. Red ribbons were attached to his head and wrists to mark his achievement. The victors were immortalised as living Gods, their legends cemented by winning in successive Games. The best were remembered in the valley of Olympia, with inscriptions carved on statues in their likeness.

All athletes swore an oath on a slice of boar's flesh that they would not sin against the Games. For ten months before the next Olympiad they trained in a strict manner, vowed not to take bribes, and promised to compete fairly.

The judges were drawn from the local Elean people. Their athletes were still allowed to compete because the Eleans had a reputation for fairness, though bribery amongst other peoples was common. According to the rules, corruption of a judge or opponent would result in the athlete's disqualification and subsequent whipping. Fines were also imposed, the money being used to build statues of Zeus.

All male Greek citizens were allowed to enter the Games, regardless of their social standing. There were separate cate-

gories for men and boys. Married women were not permitted
to enter or even to watch. Unmarried women, however, were
allowed to attend, but could not compete.

Some women dressed as men to enter the arena. If they were
caught, the rules stated that they should be thrown from the
summit of Mount Typaion. Callipateira disguised herself as a
gymnastic trainer and brought her son Peisirodus to the Games.
He won, but as she joined him in the winners' enclosure she
bared herself and was discovered. In a rare display of compas-
sion she was allowed to go free out of respect to her father,
brothers and son, all of whom had won Olympic titles. Instead,
a law was passed forcing all future trainers to strip before they
entered the arena!

The Herean Games (named after Zeus' wife Hera) were also
held every four years. Women competed, though the races were
shorter. There were at least three other athletic meetings held
every 2-4 years. The Isthmean Games were held at Corinth, the
Pythian Games at Delphi and the Nemean Games at Nemea.
The Olympics, however, predated these by over two hundred
years and remained the elite competition until the reign of
Theodosius. Polycles won the four-horse chariot race at all four
meetings.

It was not unusual for the victors to receive their meals for free,
to be given front row seats in the theatres and other public festi-
vals, to be tax exempt, and even to have private gymnasia built
for them.

The *stade*, a 192 metre sprint, was the only event for the first 13
Olympiads. The first recorded male champion was nude runner
Koroibos of Elis, traditionally dated to 776 BC. At the next

Games the *diaulos* (two *stades*) was introduced. The first distance events (*dolichos*) appeared in the 15th Games and were between seven and 24 *stades*.

Astylos of Kroton (a Greek town in southern Italy) won six sprint olive wreaths in three consecutive Olympiads (488, 484 & 480 BC) but in the latter two Games he competed for Syracuse. So incensed were the people of Kroton that they destroyed his statue and turned his house into a prison. This switching of allegiance was not uncommon: at the 98th Olympiad Sotodes won *dolichos* for Crete. At the next Games he proclaimed himself Ephesian – having been bribed by their people – and was banished from Crete for life.

Milon, also of Kroton, and a student of Pythagoras, became a six-time wrestling champion, winning his first wreath in 540 BC and his last at the 67th Olympiad in 512 BC. This is a unique achievement, even by today's standards.

Leonidas of Rhodes won the *stade*, *diaulos* and armour sprint races at four consecutive Olympics, for a total of twelve wreaths. The armour race required the athlete to run 2-4 *stades* wearing helmet, shield and greaves weighing nearly 60lbs.

Some records list Kyniska, daughter of Spartan King Archidamos, as the first female champion. Her chariot won the four horse event in 396 and 392 BC. In the equestrian events the victory wreath (*Kotinos*) went to the owner, not the rider, as they could afford the training equipment. Pausinias claims the first female to manage a chariot winner was in fact Belistiche, a woman from the seaboard of Macedonia.

Until 684 BC the Games were held in a single day. They were extended to three days, and then to five days during the fifth century. A sacrifice of 100 oxen was made to Zeus on the middle day.

Jason, of Argonauts fame, is commonly attributed with inventing the pentathlon, which became a sport in 708 BC. It comprised the *stade*, two *stades* and *dolichos* (usually 20 *stades*), the long jump, discus, wrestling and javelin. In the long jump, athletes carried weights (*Halteres*) which could be thrown backwards before landing to increase distance. The discus was made from stone, lead or iron, and the technique used then has survived almost unchanged to the present day. The wrestlers fought until one admitted defeat. Biting and genital holds were illegal, though breaking an opponent's fingers was perfectly acceptable! Aristotle described the pentathletes as the most beautiful of all competitors, with "bodies capable of enduring all efforts, either of the racecourse or of bodily strength."

Boxers used hard straps (*Himantes*) to protect their hands and fingers, but these caused terrible injuries to their opponents' faces.

According to legend the sport of *pankration* (a martial art mixing boxing and wrestling) was developed by Theseus to defeat the Minotaur. The philosopher Plato won the *pankration* title twice. Other notable participants included Socrates, Pythagoras, Aristotle and Hippocrates.

The marathon was not one of the ancient Olympic events. The myth originates from the story of the Persian invasion of Greece in the 5th century. The Persian army landed at Marathon, a small town approximately 25 miles from Athens.

The Greeks were so outnumbered that they sent messengers to towns all over the country asking for help. According to legend, Phidippides ran back to Athens to announce a Greek victory and promptly died from the exertion. It seems more likely that he was actually sent to Sparta for help, while his story has become confused with that of Eukles, who died on reaching Athens with news of the Greek victory. Phidippides' story, however, has persisted and has become the basis for the modern-day marathon.

By the 2nd century AD, the Roman Empire contributed a large number of competitors giving the Games an international flavour.

According to historical records, an army dispatched by Emperor Theodosius II destroyed the Olympic stadium in 426 AD. Over the next 1500 years natural erosive processes buried the site.

The ruins of ancient Olympia were excavated by German archaeologist Ernst Curtius between 1875 and 1881.

XXème ANNIVERSAIRE DU RÉTABLISSEMENT
DES JEUX OLYMPIQUES

1894   1914

THE MODERN GAMES

The Greeks, Swedes and even the British tried and failed to revive the Olympic movement in the 19th century. A Frenchman would eventually have greater success. Born on New Year's Day, 1863, Baron Pierre de Coubertin, a French aristocrat, was just seven years old when France was overrun by the Germans during the Franco-Prussian war. Studying the war in school, he attributed their defeat to a lack of vigour – gained through regular exercise – and not to military failings.

He studied the education systems in Britain, the United States and Germany and concluded that, on leaving school, their children were physically stronger and fitter. In 1890 he founded the Union des Societes Francaises de Sports Athletiques (USFSA). Two years later, at a Union meeting in Paris, de Coubertin proposed plans to continue the Games. "Let us export our oarsmen, our runners, our fencers into other lands….so that we may attempt to realise, upon a basis suitable to the conditions of modern life, the splendid and beneficent task of reviving the Olympic Games."

His idea was ignored, but de Coubertin was persistent. In 1892 he organised a meeting with 79 representatives from 12 countries. This time his speech was greeted with interest. They voted unanimously to revive the Games and appointed de Coubertin the task of founding a committee to oversee its running. This would evolve into the International Olympic Committee (IOC), with Demetrious Vikelas as its first president. The city of Athens was chosen as the first venue for the modern Games.

TABLE: MODERN
OLYMPIC TIMELINE

1800–1890: International efforts to restore the Olympic
Games fail.
1890: Baron Pierre de Coubertin founds USFSA to
physically educate French children.
1892: De Coubertin outlines plans for International
Olympic Committee to delegates from 12 countries.
1894: First session of IOC awards Athens the first modern
Olympic Games. They will be held at four year intervals.
1896: Games open with 300 athletes representing 14
nations. Spyros Samaras and Costis Palamas compose
Olympic Hymn, which is played during the flag raising
ceremony.
1900: First women compete in Paris.
1904: IOC decides to hold events two years after every
Olympics. They are scheduled for Athens in 1906 to
mark the tenth anniversary of the modern Games.
1906: Athens hosts Intercalated (unofficial) Games. Medals
won are not recognised by the IOC. The city states its
intention to hold the interim Games permanently.
1908: De Coubertin adapts Bishop Talbot's congratulatory
speech into the Olympic Creed. London holds first
Olympic opening ceremony.
1910: Political unrest in Greece forces the cancellation of
the interim Games and the idea is discontinued.
1912: Electric timing, a public address system for the
benefit of the spectators, and chalk instead of cord to
divide lanes on the track are all introduced in
Stockholm.

1914: De Coubertin designs Olympic flag.

1920: Olympic flag flown for the first time in Antwerp. De Coubertin penned Olympic Oath taken for the first time. He also outlines the Olympic Charter.

1921: De Coubertin pens Olympic motto –"*Citius, Altius, Fortius*"– meaning Faster, Higher, Stronger.

1924: De Coubertin retires. Radio broadcasts announce Paris results – another first. A primitive closing (flag raising) ceremony is held. First winter Olympics held in Chamonix.

1928: Against medical opinion, women are allowed to compete in track and field events for the first time. Olympic flame burns for the duration of the Amsterdam Games.

1932: Cameras accurate to $1/100^{th}$ of a second are used to provide evidence in tight finishes. The winners' rostrum, medal- and flag raising ceremonies are all introduced.

1936: The Berlin Games are covered by television for the first time. Telex services wire the results around the world.

1948: First Stoke Mandeville Games held in England. They are hailed as the blueprint for the Paralympics.

1952: The Soviet Union sends a team to the summer Olympics in Helsinki for the first time in 40 years.

1956: First official closing ceremony held in Melbourne. First winter Games to be televised in Cortina.

1957: Olympic Hymn is declared the official song of the Games.

1960: First official Paralympic Games held in Rome.

1964: Computerised scoring used first in Tokyo.

1967: IOC draws up list of banned substances.

1968: Drug testing in general – as well as sex tests for women – are introduced in Mexico City. A number of

high-profile female athletes fail to compete. First
truly synthetic (tartan) track used.

1972: 11 Israeli athletes murdered by terrorists in
Munich, but the Games go on. Officials take
Olympic Oath.

1976: First winter Paralympic Games held in Sweden.

1980: 62 countries boycott Moscow Olympics in
protest at their invasion of Afghanistan.

1984: China sends a team to the Los Angeles Games for
the first time in 52 years. John Williams composes
the "Olympic Fanfare and Theme."

1988: Professional athletes are officially invited to the
Games for the first time. Canadian Ben Johnson
becomes the highest profile athlete to be caught by
the drug testers having just won the men's 100 metres.

1992: South African athletes compete for the first time
in 32 years. German athletes compete under one flag
for the first time since 1964. The Soviet Union
enters a single team for the last time.

1994: Winter Olympic schedule altered to fit between
summer Games.

1996: A terrorist bomb kills one and injures 111 at an
Olympic concert in Atlanta.

2000: IOC President Juan Antonio Samaranch
proclaims Sydney as "The best Games ever."

2004: Athens organisers silence doubters by having all
facilities ready on time.

2005: In being awarded the 2012 Games by delegates in
Singapore, London will become the first city in the
world to host the Olympics three times (Athens
1906 being not officially recognised). IOC President
Jacques Rogge calls for the summer Games to be
limited to 28 sports, 301 events and a maximum of
10,500 athletes.

Today there are 116 IOC members who must vote to decide the venue for each summer and winter Olympics. (The IOC always awards the event to a city, never a country). There are usually five candidate cities, chosen by an IOC executive board from a list of all applicant cities (submitted by their respective National Olympic Committees) based on both their answers to a questionnaire covering various themes, and their merits discussed by a group of IOC experts. Once the city has been chosen as a candidate it must submit a file in response to a second IOC questionnaire, which will be analysed by an Evaluation Commission, and then it must host a four-day inspection visit. The Commission will then report its findings to the IOC at a general assembly. At the next IOC session, the candidate cities present their case individually and wait for a final report by the Chairperson of the Evaluation Commission. Then the voting can begin.

The candidate city with the fewest votes after each round of a secret ballot is eliminated, while the rest progress until there is a single city with a clear majority. If two cities are tied for last place a runoff election is held between them with the winner progressing to the next round. This means it is possible for a city to be in third or fourth place, survive a vote, then gain extra votes from an eliminated city's backers and win the contest.

ATHENS, 1896

The Games opened in front of 60,000 spectators at the foot of the Acropolis on the 6th of April 1896. It was the 75th anniversary of Greek independence from Turkey. Events included the sprints, shot put, pole vault, fencing, weight lifting, swimming, cycling, shooting, tennis, marathon and gymnastics. The first modern champion was James Connolly (USA). He took gold in the hop, step and jump, now called the triple jump.

To be considered eligible to enter the Games, amateur athletes had to respect the spirit of fair play and non-violence, and be a

SUMMER OLYMPICS

Year	Venue	Nations	Sports	Even
1896	Athens (Greece)	14	9	52
1900	Paris (France)	24	18	95
1904	St. Louis (USA)	12	17	91
1906	Athens (Greece–unofficial)	20	14	79
1908	London (Great Britain)	22	19	110
1912	Stockholm (Sweden)	28	14	102
1916	Not held			
1920	Antwerp (Belgium)	29	22	154
1924	Paris (France)	44	17	126
1928	Amsterdam (Netherlands)	46	14	109
1932	Los Angeles (USA)	37	14	117
1936	Berlin (Germany)	49	19	129
1940	Not held			
1944	Not held			
1948	London (Great Britain)	59	17	136
1952	Helsinki (Finland)	69	17	149
1956	Melbourne (Australia)	72	17	145
1960	Rome (Italy)	83	17	150
1964	Tokyo (Japan)	93	19	163
1968	Mexico City (Mexico)	112	20	172
1972	Munich (Germany)	121	23	195
1976	Montreal (Canada)	92	21	198
1980	Moscow (USSR)	80	21	203
1984	Los Angeles (USA)	140	23	221
1988	Seoul (South Korea)	159	25	237
1992	Barcelona (Spain)	169	28	257
1996	Atlanta (USA)	197	26	271
2000	Sydney (Australia)	200	28	300
2004	Athens (Greece)	202	28	301
2008	Beijing (China)			
2012	London (Great Britain)			

Athletes M/F	Medals	Tickets/TV figs
300/0	Greece 47	80,000
1203/22	France 102	
639/6	USA 238	2000
870/7	France 40	
1971/37	GB 145	400,000+
2359/48	Sweden 65	
2561/65	USA 95	
2954/135	USA 99	625,000
2606/277	USA 56	
1206/126	USA 103	1,250,000
3632/331	Germany 89	4,500,000
3714/390	USA 84	★500,000
4436/519	USA 76	
2938/376	USSR 98	
4727/611	USSR 99	
4473/678	USSR 96	
4735/781	USA 107	
6075/1059	USSR 99	
4824/1260	USSR 125	500 million
4064/1115	USSR 195	
5263/1566	USA 174	2.5 billion
6197/2194	USSR 132	
6652/2704	Unified 112	
6806/3512	USA 101	
6582/4069	USA 97	3.6 billion
6858/4241	USA 103	4.5 billion

★ Denotes TV audience figures used from 1948-present day.

national of the country they represented. These rules have been changed over the years to incorporate professional athletes. All participants must refrain from using substances and procedures prohibited by the rules of the IOC, as well as complying with the anti-doping code. There are nearly 100,000 Olympians alive today.

The most popular winner in Athens was Spyridon Louys, a young Greek post office messenger and shepherd, who placed first in the marathon. The Crown Princes leaped from the Royal Box to accompany him on his last lap of the track. He famously declined Games financier Georgios Averoff's daughter's hand in marriage immediately afterwards.

Since the Games had not been well publicised, many athletes had to pay for their own travel arrangements and were often not selected on ability. Some competitors turned out to be wealthy tourists who happened to be on holiday in Athens at the time!

The American team dominated the track, winning nine of the 12 events. The discus winner, Bob Garrett, had never even seen a discus before he arrived.

PARIS, 1900

At the time of the 1900 Games, Paris was also hosting the World Exhibition. As a result de Coubertin and the IOC lost control of the organisation and the Games were poorly admin- istered. More athletes attended the Games than in 1896 but conditions were awful. Some athletes were not even aware that they were competing at the Games and many died without knowing they were Olympic champions! Problems over athletes' participation exist today as many countries present inaccurate data to the event organisers.

Schedules conflicted so badly that many competitors never

made it to their events. Athletes had to run on a poorly marked
grass track, while swimmers swam in the Seine. There wasn't
even enough room in the stadium for the discus and hammer
throwers and their implements frequently landed in the
trees outside the track. There were similar problems for the
spectators, many of whom thought they were watching
the World Exhibition. The event was also overshadowed by the
opening of the new Eiffel Tower.

For the first time women were allowed to compete in Paris.
The 22 athletes contested five sports: tennis, equestrianism,
croquet, sailing and golf.

Four Americans dominated the 23 track and field events. Ray
Ewry, Alvin Kraenzlein (who was punched by rival Meyer
Prinstein during the long jump final), John Tewksbury and
Irving Baxter took 11 firsts and five seconds between them.

There were no gold medals given to winners in Paris.
Champions received silver while second placed athletes won
bronze.

> *"And here's Moses Kiptanui – the 19 year old Kenyan*
> *who turned 20 a few weeks ago"*
> David Coleman

ST. LOUIS, 1904

The third modern Games were to have been held in Chicago
but were reassigned to St. Louis at the request of President
Roosevelt. The event suffered from many of the same problems
that had befallen Paris as the city was also hosting the 100th
anniversary celebrations for the Louisiana Purchase Exhibition.
To accommodate the exhibition the Olympics were held
between July and November, but they were so disorganised that
only 2000 spectators attended.

Marathon runner Fred Lorz (USA) suffered terrible cramp during the race. He flagged down a helpful motorist and was driven 11 miles towards the stadium. He ran the last five miles and was hailed as the winner by confused officials. The truth was discovered just before he was crowned with the traditional olive wreath when Alice Roosevelt, the president's daughter, produced a photo of him accepting the lift. Thomas Hicks (USA) was eventually given the gold but he had to be fed a cocktail of strychnine and cognac to ease the pain of terrible blisters in the overpowering heat. Banned for life, Lorz was reinstated a year later and won the 1905 Boston Marathon.

Len Tau and Jan Mashiani became the first African Olympians.

Holding the Games so far from Europe limited the number of participants, many of whom did not want to make the trans-Atlantic voyage followed by a gruelling train journey to a small town on the wilderness frontier. Only about 100 of the 645 competitors were from outside the USA. The rest came from Canada, with no representatives at all from France, Sweden or England. The USA won 80% of the medals as a result, including 23 of 25 on the track.

"Tahamata went through the air like a torpedo"
Peter Jones

ATHENS, 1906

The IOC had decided that there should be competitions between every Olympics. In 1906, these were held in Athens (which planned to hold all intermediate Games thereafter), but they are now recognised as the unofficial or Intercalated Games. Due to political unrest in Greece in 1910, this idea was discontinued. However, it should be noted that after the poor organisation of the previous two Olympics, the Athens Games very possibly saved the movement from extinction. In fact the only complaint seemed to be over the soft cinder track.

Verner Jarvinen (Finland) won the Greek-style discus and came second in the freestyle event. He returned home a national hero and encouraged his country to take a more active role in the Olympic movement.

The javelin and the pentathlon were added to the program of events. The latter saw athletes compete in a 192 metre (*stade*) run, standing long jump, discus and javelin throws, and Greco-Roman wrestling, the idea being to revive the spirit of the ancient Games. It was won by Swede Hjalmar Mellander.

> *"For those of you watching who do not have television sets,*
> *live commentary is on Radio 2"*
> David Coleman

LONDON, 1908

The 1908 Olympics were scheduled for Rome, but the eruption of Mount Vesuvius forced organisers to choose a different city at the last minute: London. Although the Games were well organised, they were tainted by politics. The Irish boycotted proceedings because they had been refused independence, while the American team refused to lower their flag to the Royal Family during the opening ceremony. This was in protest at there being no American flag decorating the new 68,000 capacity stadium in Shepherd's Bush. The US team upholds this tradition today. Ruled by Russia, the Finnish team were not allowed their own flag and marched without one in protest.

During the opening ceremony the Greek team are always presented first. The remainder follow in alphabetical order (in the language of the host country), except for the hosts themselves, who appear last.

Bishop Ethelbert Talbot wrote a speech for all champions at the 1908 Games. De Coubertin adapted it to form the Olympic Creed, which reads: "The important thing about the Olympic

Games is not to win but to take part, just as the important thing
in life is not the triumph but the struggle. The essential thing is
not to have conquered but to have fought well."

As the Royal Family couldn't see the marathon start line, the
race was extended by a mile so that it began outside Windsor
Castle. Then, at the insistence of Princess Mary, the start was
moved beneath the windows of the Royal Nursery (a further
385 yards), making the overall distance 26 miles and 385 yards
(ratified in 1924). Over a quarter of a million Londoners turned
out to watch the event. The race ended in controversy, however,
as Italian Dorando Pietri was helped to his feet four times
before being escorted over the winning line by officials, including
one Arthur Conan Doyle. American Johnny Hayes was declared
the winner after heated arguments between officials and the US
team. Fights broke out in the stands during the delay. Pietri
spent several hours with serious heat exhaustion and would
have died had he not been rushed to hospital. His exploits
ensured he became the most famous athlete of the time. Queen
Alexandra gave him a gold cup and Irving Berlin immortalised
him in song.

Ray Ewry (USA) completed a remarkable career by winning
his 10th gold medal. He was rarely beaten in the standing-,
triple- and long jumps and set an outright record that would
remain unchallenged for more than three quarters of a century.
And all this from a man who had polio as a child.

In the 400 metres final British officials voided the result (a USA
one-two) citing illegal blocking by John Carpenter on the
British runner Wyndham Halswelle. The Americans refused to
re-run the race and Halswelle collected the gold. The two
countries clashed again when officials refused to allow the US
track team manager onto the field.

The Canadians complained that the cycling track was too steep
and that English food was awful. Then the Swedes jumped in

to complain about the wrestling judging and the French attacked the cycling officials. And it rained constantly for the entire Games! In response to the criticism, the IOC ruled that officials could no longer be supplied by the host country.

John Taylor (USA) became the first black athlete to win a gold medal (medley relay), while marksmen Oscar and Alfred Swahn (Sweden) became the first father and son team to take gold.

> *"It's a great advantage being able to hurdle with both legs"*
> David Coleman

STOCKHOLM, 1912

Avery Brundage, president of the IOC from 1952-1972, described the 1912 Games in Stockholm as the most efficient and well-organised Games of all. This was due largely to the new 22,000 seat stadium, swimming pools and athletes' accommodation. The Swedes also shortened the program to just two months and refused to allow any other event to be held

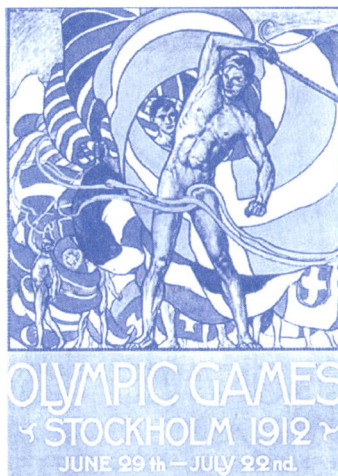

concurrently. The Games were the first to attract massive media attention, with events making front page news in the US and UK. Some sports (notably boxing, which was illegal in Sweden) were dropped.

Jim Thorpe (USA) won the pentathlon and decathlon. As King Gustav presented him with his medal he called him the greatest athlete in the world. Thorpe is said to have replied, "Thanks, King!" It later emerged that he had played semi-professional baseball in the 1909-10 season and the IOC stripped him of his medals. They were restored, along with his records, in 1982, 29 years after his death.

Portugal's Francisco Lazaro collapsed during the marathon and died the next day. Danish cyclist Knud Enemark Jensen is the only other athlete to die during an Olympic event (1964).

Hawaiian Duke Paoa Kahanamoku won the 100 metres freestyle in the pool by pioneering the front crawl stroke.

After 1912 the gold medals were no longer made entirely from gold. They must now contain only six grams of the metal. At least three millimetres thick and sixty in diameter, silver medals must contain 92.5% silver. The design on each colour medal is up to the host city's organising committee, but must be approved by the IOC.

> *"This is a very well balanced football match.*
> *Of course one side or the other will eventually win"*
> Jim Rosenthal

The 1916 Games were to have been held in Berlin but the world was at war and they were cancelled.

ANTWERP, 1920

Though Germany, Austria and Hungary were not forbidden to
come to the 1920 Games in Antwerp, Belgium, they were not
formally invited and did not send teams. (The Soviet Union
wouldn't do so until 1952.) Incessant rain made track
conditions difficult and the athletes bunked in abandoned
schoolhouses. The American team almost pulled out in protest.

One of the greatest athletes of all time emerged in 1920.
Paavo Nurmi, the flying Finn, won the first of his nine distance
running gold- and three silver medals. He would also take gold
in 1924 and 1928.

Flown for the first time, the Olympic flag consists of five inter-
connected rings on a white background. The rings signify the
five main continents (Africa, America, Asia, Australia and
Europe) and are connected to promote peace and friendship.
They are coloured (left to right) blue, yellow, black, green and
red. These colours were chosen because at least one appears on
the flag of every country in the world.

The Olympic Oath was first taken by Belgian fencer Victor
Bion. It reads: "In the name of all competitors, I promise that
we shall take part in these Olympic Games, respecting and
abiding by the rules that govern them, in the true spirit of
sportsmanship, for the glory of sport and honour of our teams."

De Coubertin's Olympic Charter outlined his idea to build a
peaceful, better world by educating the youth through sport
without discrimination. Today the IOC's essential missions are
to choose the host city, organise the Games, promote women in
sport, protect all athletes and the environment, and respect the
Olympic Truce.

JEVX OLYMPIQVES
PARIS 1924

PARIS, 1924

With Pierre de Coubertin retiring, the 1924 Games were held in Paris in his honour. They were originally scheduled for Amsterdam but he insisted the French capital have a chance to make up for the 1900 fiasco. The French built the superb 60,000 seat stadium Colombes, a basic Olympic village and a swimming pool complex. Over 1000 journalists covered the action.

Winter sports were added to the list of events and were con-tested in January and February. (The tradition of holding the winter sports a few months earlier ended in 1992. See Winter Olympics).

The exploits of Harold Abrahams (gold in the 100 metres) and Eric Liddell (gold in the 400 metres) at the Paris Games are immortalised in the Academy Award winning film *Chariots of Fire* (1981). Though the story is based on fact, Liddell knew long before the Games that his 100 metre heats would take place on a Sunday. A devout Christian, he decided not to compete and changed to the 400 metres. The two never raced each other in real life.

Three flags were raised on the last day of competition, that of the IOC, the host nation and the next host nation.

"And with an alphabetical irony, Nigeria follows New Zealand"
David Coleman

AMSTERDAM, 1928

There were more scandals at the 1928 Games. Queen Wilhelmine denounced the event as a Pagan festival and refused to attend the opening ceremony. Dutch officials insisted that a track and field program for women was included, but both de Coubertin and the Vatican lobbied against it. Some even claimed that women would have to become more masculine and could ruin their health or prevent themselves from having children by competing. The British team heeded the warnings and didn't send a female contingent. Incidentally, six of the women who finished the 800 metres collapsed at the finish line and the event was dropped. It was only reinstated, along with all other distances over 200 metres, 32 years later. Also, the German team was invited back after an eighteen year absence.

All other team members had to be satisfied with a sleeping bag in the army barracks for accommodation as there was no Olympic village. Once again the American team objected to the conditions and they hired two boats in Amsterdam harbour to house their athletes.

Johnny Weissmuller (USA), who played Tarzan on the big screen after retiring from sport, took five gold medals in the pool (1924-28) and a bronze for water polo.

In ancient times, the Olympic flame was ignited by the sun and kept alight for the duration of the Games. It made a reappearance at the 1928 Games, representing purity and the striving for perfection. Chairman of the organising committee of the 1936 Games, Carl Diem suggested the idea for the Torch relay. Having been lit at Olympia, the Torch was then carried by men and women runners to the host city and represented the continuation of the Games from ancient to modern times.

"She's not Ben Johnson – but then who is?"
David Coleman

LOS ANGELES, 1932

The Los Angeles Games in 1932 almost didn't happen. Most countries took their time replying to the official invitations as they were all struggling financially in the middle of the Great Depression. As a result, organisers cut the duration of competition to just 16 days (now the standard). The city also constructed an extensive Olympic Village. The men were housed in Baldwin Hills and the women in the Chapman Park Hotel downtown. The organisers also built a 10,000 seat swimming park and a cycling track in the Pasadena Rose Bowl.

Sixteen world and Olympic records fell in men's track and field, Jim Thorpe's decathlon record of 6845 points being finally beaten by James Bausch. It had stood for 20 years.

American "Babe" Mildred Didrikson Zaharias became the Games' heroine. She won gold in the 80 metre hurdles in a new world record, gold in the javelin and silver in the high jump. Retiring from the sport aged just 18, she went on to become a successful tennis player and the finest golfer in the world, winning 17 titles in a single year (1947).

"This is a really lovely horse, and I speak from
personal experience as I once mounted her mother"
Ted Walsh

BERLIN, 1936

The 1936 Olympics had been awarded to Berlin two years before Hitler had marched to power, and there was international pressure to boycott the Games in protest at his anti-Semitic policies. The Nazis used the event to promote their 'superior' Aryan Race, building four stadiums, swimming pools and an extensive Olympic Village, which was patrolled by the German secret police (*Gestapo*). In fact the Nazi war song "*Horst Wessel Lied*" was played nearly 500 times during the event. All athletes were supposed to shout "*Seig Heil*" and salute when they passed Hitler at the opening ceremony but, as usual, the Americans objected and were roundly booed by the crowd.

At their peak, closed circuit TV audiences at 28 locations around the capital reached 150,000.

The star of the show was undoubtedly the "Ebony Express" Jesse Owens. His rise to superstardom had been meteoric. On the afternoon of 25th May 1935, at the finals of the US track and field championships, he set world records in the 100 yards (9.4 seconds), the long jump (26 feet 8 and a quarter inches – 8.13m), the 220 yards and the 220 yards hurdles. In so doing, he also set a world best time for the 200 metres! All of these world records were set in just 45 minutes, with the long jump mark standing for over 25 years. And he was a smoker!

At the Olympics he collected four gold medals (100- and 200 metres, long jump and sprint relay), beating stiff German competition in every round. Adolf Hitler famously refused to shake his hand, though why this happened is not clear. Some believe that it was because Owens was black and did not conform to Hitler's idea of white racial superiority, while others are less sure, citing IOC President Henri de Baillet-Latour's suggestion that Hitler should not congratulate any athlete on the track for fear of breaching Olympic guidelines.

The 1940 Games were to have been held in Tokyo but Japan
was seen as an aggressive country with powerful military goals
and they were rescheduled for Helsinki. The outbreak of World
War Two in 1939 forced organisers to cancel the Games, with
the 1944 event suffering the same fate.

LONDON, 1948

Deciding to hold the next Games in London was considered a
bold move. Much of Europe had been ravaged by war and its
people were very poor. All those invited had to supply food for
their own athletes (housed either in military camps or colleges) and
no new facilities were built. As usual, the Americans revolted:
they imported 42 tons of meat, 36 tons of cheese and 25,000
chocolate bars. Thankfully Wembley had survived the war and
proved a popular venue for the track and field events, but many
more venues had to be rebuilt. Germany and Japan were not
invited to compete.

The media were to have a significant impact on the Games'
popularity. 250 broadcasters presented radio shows in 40 lan-
guages, the technological advances made during the war helping to build a worldwide communications network.

There was confusion and the usual Anglo-American controversy after the sprint relay. The judges ruled that the American
team, which had appeared to win comfortably, had actually
exchanged the baton outside the marked area. Their medals
were presented to the Great Britain team after they were disqualified. They were reinstated as Olympic Champions once
photos proved the pass was in fact legal.

The star of the show was Dutch woman Fanny Blankers-Koen.
Her husband thought her too old to compete but she defied the
critics to win the 100- and 200metres, and 80 metres hurdles.
She also guided the relay team to gold after coming off the last
bend in fourth place. During her career she set 12 world records.

"Morcelli has the four fastest 1500 metre times ever, and all at 1500 metres"
David Coleman

OFFICIAL SOUVENIR

American Bob Mathias won the decathlon at 17, just four months after taking up the event. He quipped afterwards that his next goal was to start shaving! He would become the first man to successfully defend the title in Helsinki.

HELSINKI, 1952

Legends Paavo Nurmi and Hannes Kolehmainen exchanged the Olympic baton at the opening ceremony. The Soviet Union sent athletes to the 1952 Games in Helsinki for the first time in forty years but their coaches kept them segregated from the other competitors. It was a wonder they were invited; the Soviet army had invaded Finland twice during World War Two.

Russian gymnast Maria Gorokhovskaya became the only woman to win seven medals at a single Olympics (two gold and five silver).

Emil Zatopek (Czechoslovakia) successfully defended his

10,000 metres title, then won the 5000 metres and the marathon—an event he'd never run—and each in Olympic record time. His wife, Dana Zatopkova, won the women's javelin, also with an Olympic record.

MELBOURNE, 1956

The Melbourne Games in 1956 were the first to be held in the southern hemisphere, indeed the first outside the USA or Europe. The event was held in November and December to coincide with the Australian summer. However, due to Australia's strict quarantine laws the equestrian events were held in Stockholm.

The Suez Crisis forced Egypt, Iran and Lebanon to boycott the Games, while the Netherlands, Spain and Switzerland refused to send teams in protest at the Soviet invasion of Hungary. Russia met Hungary in the water polo semi-finals, with the Hungarian team winning easily (4-0). Players and fans had to be separated after a brawl following a Soviet head-butt.

Australia's Dawn Fraser took the first of her three successive 100 metre freestyle titles, while compatriot Murray Rose took the first of his two.

Possibly the greatest discus thrower of them all, Al Oerter (USA) won Olympic gold. He won again in Rome and Tokyo, and completed an outstanding twelve year stay at the top of his sport by taking gold in Mexico in 1968, the first person to win four consecutive gold medals in the same event.

> *"He's 31 this year – last year he was 30"*
> David Coleman

> *"It was the fastest ever swim over that distance on American soil"*
> Greg Phillips

ROME, 1960

De Coubertin had always favoured Rome as a venue for the Olympics. Television cameras covered every sport with a number of important historical sites hosting individual events – the wrestling at the Basilica of Maxentius and the gymnastics at the Baths of Caracalla.

Arguably the most famous sportsman to have lived, some say the most recognisable person in history, Cassius Clay, who became Muhammad Ali, won a gold medal in the light heavyweight boxing. He was so proud of the achievement that he wore the medal solidly for two days! He famously threw it in the Ohio River a year later after being refused service in a segregated restaurant.

Hungarian fencer Gerevich Aladar won his sixth consecutive Olympic gold medal in the team event (1932-1960).

One of 22 children, sprinter Wilma Rudolph (USA) couldn't walk unaided until she was nine years old after crippling bouts of scarlet fever, polio and pneumonia. She won the 100- and 200 metres and anchored the relay team to her third gold medal. Running barefoot, Abebe Bikila (Ethiopia) won the marathon. He won it again four years later and went home to a State reception.

> *"There goes Juantorena down the back straight,*
> *opening his legs and showing his class"*
> David Coleman

TOKYO, 1964

South African athletes were not invited to compete in the first Asian Games as their government supported the policy of apartheid. Indonesian and North Korean teams withdrew after

MONEY MATTERS
HOW THE FINANCES OF THE GAMES
HAVE CHANGED

1896: The Greek government, which had been unable to fund a new stadium, accepts a gift of over one million drachmas from architect Georgios Averoff to restore the Panathenaic Stadium in white marble. Crown Prince Constantine also contributes by marketing Olympic stamps and medals.

1909-10: Jim Thorpe (USA) is paid $15 to play major league baseball for a season.

1912: Thorpe is stripped of his Stockholm Olympic medals as he is judged by the IOC to be a professional sportsman.

1920: Most people cannot afford tickets to watch events at the Antwerp Games and spectator numbers are low. The Belgian economy eventually loses over half a billion francs from hosting the Olympics.

1924: Tennis is recognised as a professional game and is removed from the list of Olympic sports.

1932: Organisers issue a three-cent Olympic stamp to generate revenue for the Los Angeles Games in the midst of the Great Depression. Douglas Fairbanks, Marlene Dietrich, Gary Cooper and Charlie Chaplin perform alongside 3000 singers, dancers and musicians to entertain the crowds. Spectators pack the 105,000 seat Memorial Coliseum stadium every day and the Games turn a profit of $1 million. Having been paid to run in Europe, Paavo Nurmi is deemed to have turned professional and is barred from competing. Athlete Mildred "Babe" Didrikson turns to professional tennis and golf.

1936: The Berlin Olympic stadium is built at a cost of $25 million. Organisers sell nearly five million tickets. Winter Olympian Sonja Henie (Norway) moves to the USA and turns professional, touring the country with her own skating

show. When she dies in 1969 she has starred in a number of
major motion pictures and is reported to be worth $45
million.

1948: Still struggling in the aftermath of the war London spends
as little as possible on hosting the Games. They end up costing
£600,000 and turn a profit of just £10,000. The BBC pays
the equivalent of $3000 for the broadcasting rights.

1960: CBS buys the broadcasting rights for the Rome Olympics
for $394,000.

1964: Tokyo spends over $3 billion rebuilding before the Games.

1972: Munich spends $650 million on facilities and repairing
bomb damage still evident from the war. Austrian skier Karl
Schranz is deemed to have turned professional, reportedly
earning over $50,000 a year for testing skis with sponsors'
logos on them. Avery Brundage forbids him from entering
the Sapporo Games but allows nearly forty other "semi-
professionals" to compete. The controversy surrounding
Schranz is not confined to the skiing: Canada refuses to send
an ice hockey team protesting against the use of professional
amateurs by Russia and the eastern bloc.

1976: The Montreal Games are fraught with financial and
political problems. Quebec alone spends more then $2 billion
on new facilities and promotion (up from an original estimate
of $124 million). They leave themselves debt ridden for more
than twenty years. The Olympic stadium ends up costing $485
million and the roof isn't even finished. $100 million is spent
on security after the terrorist attack in Munich.

1980: NBC pays $100 million for the broadcasting rights to the
Moscow Games. President Jimmy Carter blocks the move on
the grounds that if Americans can't compete (he actually
threatens to cap all athletes' training and travelling expenses
if they try to go to Russia) the event shouldn't be shown on
television in the US. Lloyds of London are forced to reimburse
the company $90 million.

1984: Corporate sponsorship allows the Games to turn a profit
($225 million), the first to make a major return since 1932. As
a result, *Time* magazine names Games organiser Peter
Ueberroth as its man of the year. MacDonald's pay $4 million
for the naming rights to the Olympic pool! Many accuse the
Americans of selling out to the advertising companies and
ruining television coverage with too many breaks for "words
from our sponsors". Though the Games are still strictly
amateur, it is well known that many athletes are being offered
huge appearance fees and sponsorship deals with soft drinks
giants and sportswear manufacturers. Winter Olympians Jayne
Torvill and Christopher Dean (GB) take gold in the ice skating
and immediately turn professional.

1988: Professional athletes are officially allowed to compete in
Seoul for the first time. As a direct result tennis makes a
comeback. The Games are well organised and policed and
make a profit of $288 million.

1992: $8 billion is spent upgrading the city of Barcelona. With the
professional era in full swing, the USA sends a basketball
"Dream Team" made up of NBA stars. They comfortably take
the gold medal. Track and field athletes are also routinely paid
to compete, with many receiving bonuses for world records
(see Sergey Bubka, 1992).

1994: Professional ice dancers Jayne Torvill and Christopher Dean
(GB) return to Olympic competition. They narrowly miss out
on gold.

1996: Atlanta's administrative failings (see details below) cannot be
blamed on a lack of money. The event is seen as a marketing
dream with corporate logos everywhere and big name sponsors
such as Coca-Cola swamping the advertising hoardings.

2000: Though praised as the best Games ever, the Olympic park is
underused at the end of the Sydney festival and initial
optimism over the money made fades.

2001-2004: The Olympic Movement publishes its revenue
figures. Broadcast rights account for 53% percent with
$2.23 billion; sponsorship amounts to $1.46 billion;
ticketing raises $441 million and licensing official products
brings in $86.5 million.

2003: NBC pays $820 million for rights to show Vancouver
winter Olympics in 2010.

2004: $1.6 billion is spent on policing the Athens Games. This
pays for 45,000 security personnel, comprising 25,000 police,
7000 soldiers, 3000 members of the coast guard, more than
1500 fire-fighters, and 8000 private bodyguards and other
volunteers. The overall cost would rise to more than $9 billion.

2005: London outlines its proposed costs of hosting the 2012
Olympics. The £1.5 billion raised through a special Olympic
lottery, £625 million from increased council tax bills and
£250 million from the London Development Agency should
allow the city to prepare for the event. Then £800 million
will be donated by the IOC for broadcast rights, £450 million
will be generated by local sponsors, £300 million will be
made from ticket sales, as well as an extra £60 million from
licensing the event. The total bill is expected to be around
£4 billion with organisers expecting to turn a profit of £100
million, though these figures are likely to change regularly
(with the most likely outcome seeing operating and
construction costs skyrocketing and profits falling). In agreeing
to host the Games, the city has also earmarked a further £7
billion on improving its infrastructure (Channel Tunnel rail
link, East London Line extension), though this money would
have been spent regardless of the bid outcome. £695 million
will be made available for temporary transport measures such
as limousines for VIPs as well as extra tubes and buses for
athletes and spectators.

several of their athletes were disqualified for entering the New
Emerging Forces Games in Jakarta the previous year.

American Don Schollander won four individual gold medals in
the pool. Between 1963 and 1968 he set an amazing 22 world
records. Australian Dawn Fraser won the 100 metres freestyle
for the third successive Games. Her achievement is all the more
remarkable given that just before the Games she had been
involved in a car crash in which her mother was killed. The
wounds Fraser suffered appeared to be psychological as well as
physical. She was arrested trying to steal the Olympic flag from
the Imperial Palace a few days later, and although the Emperor
refused to press charges, the Australian swimming federation
suspended her for ten years, effectively ending her career.

Betty Cuthbert (Australia) returned after an eight year absence
to win the 400 metres on the track. She had won three sprint
gold medals in Melbourne. Ann Packer (GB) won the women's
800 metres, while compatriot Mary Rand won the long jump.

American sprinter Robert Lee Hayes equalled the 100 metres
world record on the track with ten seconds flat. Then he
anchored the 4x100 metre relay team to gold and a new world
record with a sub-nine second final leg.

"This boy swims like a greyhound"
Anthony Still

MEXICO CITY, 1968

These Games were almost cancelled before they began. Ten
days earlier the Mexican army opened fire on a crowd of
students protesting against the government in the Plaza of
Three Cultures. Over 250 were killed and a 1000 more wounded.
Indeed it wasn't just Mexico that was in turmoil. The Vietnam
War, the assassinations of Robert Kennedy and Martin Luther
King, and the Soviet invasion of Czechoslovakia all vied for
the news headlines.

The Olympic stadium was at an altitude of 7349 feet (2240 metres), leading some athletes to voice concerns over the low oxygen content of the air – 30% less than at sea level – which would tell in the distance races. There were no complaints from the sprinters, however. With less air resistance to slow them down they broke 34 world records. Jim Hines (USA) took gold in the 100 metres in just 9.95 seconds.

Arguably the greatest single moment in track and field history occurred when Bob Beamon (USA) hurtled down the runway in the first round of the long- jump. Such was the height of his jump that he could have cleared 1.78 metres vertically! The distance was 8.90 metres or 29 feet 2 and a half inches, nearly 2 feet beyond the old world record! Beamon himself couldn't believe what he had done, saying, "Tell me I'm not dream-ing…that's not possible…I think I'm going to be sick!" Though experts at the time predicted the record would last well into the 21st century, Carl Lewis, the great American sprinter, came close on many occasions to bettering it (his best was actually a wind-assisted leap of 8.91 metres). However, it was another American, Mike Powell, who finally eclipsed Beamon's mark with a jump 8.95 metres at the world championships in Tokyo in 1991.

Dick Fosbury (USA) turned the world of high jumping on its head, literally, when he introduced his distinctive new style, the Fosbury flop. It helped him to the gold medal.

Americans Tommie Smith and John Carlos won gold and bronze respectively in the 200 metres. During the national anthem at the medals ceremony they raised their gloved hands in a Black Power salute. They had hoped to raise awareness of the way some blacks were being treated at home but the IOC deemed their act contrary to the Games' ideals and they were expelled.

"Her legs are kept tightly together: she's giving nothing away"
BBC Gymnastics Commentator

MUNICH, 1972

The 1972 Olympics in Munich were tainted by violence. With six competitive days left, eight Palestinian terrorists seized 11 Israeli athletes inside the Olympic village. They requested the release of 234 Palestinians being held inside Israel. The request was denied and all 11 athletes as well as five terrorists were killed during a failed rescue attempt at a military airfield. Outgoing IOC president Avery Brundage declared "the Games must go on", and they did, after a delay of 24 hours. All flags were flown at half mast during a memorial service attended by 80,000 at the Olympic stadium, but the decision to continue was hugely controversial. There was also tension between the two German teams. Though the West had tried to smooth their relationship, they were wary of the East as athletic giants and both teams marched under the Olympic flag instead of their own.

Mark Spitz had his revenge on the critics who had written him off after a poor showing in Mexico. In an outstanding week he secured seven swimming gold medals with seven world records, taking his overall tally to 11 Olympic medals, nine of them gold. He was immediately advised to leave the country. As a successful American Jew he was seen as a terrorist target.

Mary Peters (GB) was a popular gold medallist in the pentathlon, while Soviet gymnast Olga Korbut won three golds and a silver.

Alan Pascoe (GB), who competed at three consecutive Olympiads, guided his 4x400 metre relay team to the silver medal on the track. He later became captain of the British team and was awarded an MBE in 1975, but his greatest challenge was to bring the 2012 Games to London as Vice-Chairman of the bidding team.

Track medallists Vince Matthews and Wayne Collett (both USA) echoed the Black Power salute and refused to stand to attention on the rostrum. The IOC ordered them out of the Olympic village and they were banned from competition for life. The basketball final provided more controversy. The US team, unbeaten in 62 Olympic matches, lost to the Soviet Union 51-50 after the Russians were given three attempts to convert a last second pass. They refused the silver medal.

MONTREAL, 1976
26 African nations boycotted the Games in protest at New Zealand's rugby tour of South Africa.

The American men dominated in the pool, winning 12 of the 13 events. Britain's David Wilkie broke their monopoly on the medals with a gold and world record in the 200 metres breast-stroke. The East German women's team took 11 of the 13 golds amid allegations of serial drug taking. A similar team had won no gold medals four years previously. It has since been revealed that many of the Eastern Bloc nations had intensive doping programmes

The brilliant 14 year-old Romanian gymnast Nadia Comaneci scored seven perfect 10s to win 3 gold medals.

Sugar Ray Leonard won boxing gold for the USA, as did the Spinks brothers, Michael and Leon.

"The Montreal Olympics can no more
have a deficit
than man can have a baby"
Mayor Jean Drapeau

MOSCOW, 1980

The first Games to be held in a Communist country, the 1980 Olympics in Moscow were also plagued with political problems. The Soviet Union had invaded Afghanistan in December 1979 and 62 countries boycotted the Games in protest. The Games were also blighted by accusations of poor judging and the crowd booed the Poles and East Germans relentlessly. So as not to subject their children to Western influences, Soviet officials called for all seven to 15 year olds to leave the city for the duration of the Games!

Gymnast Nadia Comaneci (Romania) returned to take another two golds, while the Soviet Union's Aleksandr Dityatin (also gymnastics) became the first person to win eight medals in a single year (three gold).

Sebastian Coe (GB) had been favourite to take the 800 metres gold but he misjudged the pace and was beaten by arch rival Steve Ovett (also GB). He gained his revenge in Ovett's favoured distance, the 1500 metres, in the most exciting finish of the Games. Coe would repeat his victory in the 1500 metres four years later in Los Angeles, thus becoming the first man since Jim Lightbody (USA, 1906) to successfully defend the Olympic title.

At the closing ceremony organisers were not prepared to raise the American flag as the next host nation; they raised the flag of the city of Los Angeles instead.

"This is a fascinating duel between the three men"
David Coleman

LOS ANGELES, 1984

In retaliation at their boycott four years earlier, the Soviet Union and 13 other countries failed to send teams to Los Angeles in 1984. Romania was the only Warsaw Pact country to break the mould.

Steve Redgrave (GB) won his first Olympic gold in Los Angeles. He would win his last in Sydney in 2000, a record fifth consecutive title in an endurance event and a unique achievement.

Ecaterina Szabo (Romania) won four gymnastics golds and a silver, but her achievements were almost overshadowed by tiny home favourite Mary-Lou Retton who won the women's all-round title with a pair of perfect 10s.

American Carl Lewis was the undisputed king of the track. He took gold medals in the 100 metres, 200 metres, long jump and sprint relay, the latter in a world record. His team-mate Valerie Brisco-Hooks backed him up with wins in the 200- and 400 metres and the 4x100 metre relay.

Home favourite Mary Decker tripped over Zola Budd (GB) in the final of the women's 3000 metres and couldn't continue. Although she finished, the tiny barefoot Budd was so upset by the incident that she dropped well down the field.

"Zola Budd, so small you literally can't see her, yet there she is"
Alan Parry

Francis Morgan 'Daley' Thompson (GB) proved himself to be the greatest all-rounder by taking his second decathlon title. He'd broken the world record in Moscow, and in Los Angeles became only the second man to defend the title. During the

DRUGS IN SPORT

Drug Type	Example
Anabolic Steroids	Winstrol, Nandrolone Tetrahydrogestrinone (THG)
Diuretics	Furosemide Amiloride Triamterene
Stimulants	Amphetamines Cocaine
Narcotic Analgesics	Morphine Opium Heroin Codeine
Beta-blockers	Carvedilol Metoprolol
Human Growth Hormone (Peptides)	Somatotropin Erythroprotein (EPO) Human Chorionic Gonadotrophin (HGC)
Blood Doping	Athlete removes a litre of blood and stores it, then injects it prior to competition
Cannabinoids	Cannabis and derivatives

Effect	Used In
+Helps build muscle mass, reduces fatigue, aids recovery, boosts testosterone levels -Expansion of cardiac muscle, liver damage, extreme bone growth, can increase risk of developing cancer, facial hair growth (women), breast growth (men), impotence, mood swings	Athletics Weight-lifting Rowing
+Increases urine production (weight loss), removes other banned substances from system -Can cause severe dehydration, heart arrhythmia, heat stroke, blood clots	Boxing Cricket Horse racing
+Increases alertness and heart rate, perceived reduction in fatigue -Seizure, heart attack, stroke	Cycling Athletics
+Kills pain, reduces inflammation -Sedation masks injury, addiction, gastrointestinal problems	All sports
+Lowers heart rate -Shortness of breath, fatigue, dizziness, infertility	Archery Bowls Snooker, Golf
+Practically undetectable, works like an anabolic steroid, increases oxygen carrying capacity of blood -Can damage heart, liver, kidneys, causes mutation of fingers and toes, increases cancer risk, thickening of blood, low heart rate	All sports (endurance based) Cross-country skiers
+Increases oxygen carrying capacity of blood, difficult to detect -Blood becoming contaminated, carrying extra weight, blood clots, kidney damage	Cyclists Endurance athletes Skiers
+Masks pain, increases heart rate, reduces anxiety -Paranoia, mood swings, depression, loss of coordination	All sports

pole vault in Seoul his pole snapped and ruined his chances of a third consecutive gold.

"Her best time is about 4-33, which she's definitely capable of"
David Coleman

SEOUL, 1988

North Korea boycotted the 1988 Games in Seoul because they were not allowed to co-host the event. They were joined by Ethiopia and Cuba. The relatively small number of countries staying away ensured the best Games to date.

The most famous and watched track race of all time was also the most controversial. The men's 100 metre final pitted Carl Lewis (USA) against the Canadian Ben Johnson. Johnson eased clear to win by a huge margin in 9.79 seconds, shattering his own world record. It was only after the results of a drug test were announced that the reason for his victory became clear. He had been using anabolic steroids (winstrol) to boost his performance, and had been doing so since 1984. All his records were erased and he was sent home in disgrace. He noted that as a champion he had been proudly proclaimed as Canadian by his adopted country, but after the scandal he was branded an unworthy Caribbean immigrant. Lewis was presented with the gold and Britain's Linford Christie was promoted to take the silver. Both athletes would later become embroiled in drug testing controversies.

More controversy surrounded the women's sprint races. American Florence Griffith-Joyner (Flojo) recorded world records in the heats and finals of the 200 metres. She eventually won three gold medals (100 metres, 200 metres, 4x100 metres relay). Her times still stand nearly eighteen years later but many have suggested that she, too, was using performance enhancing drugs, although when tested she never failed. Sadly

CURRENT OLYMPIC SPORTS

Archery	Equestrian	Sailing
Aquatics	Fencing	Shooting
(Swimming)	Football	Softball
Athletics	Gymnastics	Table Tennis
Badminton	Handball	Taekwondo
Baseball	Hockey	Tennis
Basketball	Judo	Triathlon
Boxing	Modern	Volleyball
Canoeing	Pentathlon	Weightlifting
Cycling	Rowing	Wrestling

Sports recognised by the IOC but not currently included in the program:

Air Sports	Bowling	Cricket
Golf (1904)	Motorcycling	Polo (1936)
Rink Hockey	Surfing	Water Skiing
Bandy	Bridge	Croquet
Karate	Netball	Power boating
Roller Sports	Sumo	Wushu
Billiards	Chess	Dance Sport
Korfball	Orienteering	Racquetball
Roque	Tug of War (1920)	Lacrosse(1948)
Boules	Climbing	
Lifesaving	Pelote Basque	*Brackets denote the*
Squash	Underwater	*year the sport was*
	Sports	*discontinued*

*"If you don't believe you can win,
there's no point getting out of bed at the end of the day"*
Neville Southall

she will never silence the doubters. She died in 1998 from a suspected heart seizure at the age of 38. Her death has fuelled further speculation that her body was ravaged by years of drug abuse.

In the pool female swimmer Kristin Otto (East Germany) won six gold medals, while American Matt Biondi won five out of a total of seven. He would win two more golds four years later.

Steffi Graf added Olympic gold to her famous tennis 'Grand Slam' for an unprecedented 'clean sweep'.

"There's Brendan Foster, all by himself with 20,000 people"
David Coleman

"This is Gregoriava from Bulgaria. I saw her snatch this morning during the warm-up and it was amazing"
NBC weight-lifting commentator Pat Glenn

BARCELONA, 1992

By 1992 the political landscape the world over had altered. The Cold War had ended, the Soviet Union no longer existed, apartheid was history and the two Germanys had united. As a result, the Games were the most eagerly anticipated and were hailed at the time as the best organised.

At 32 Linford Christie (GB) became the oldest ever 100 metres champion. He held the titles of British-, European-, Commonwealth-, World- and Olympic Champion simultaneously, the first man to do so. His team-mate Sally Gunnell won gold in the women's 400 metre hurdles.

Gail Devers (USA) took a remarkable gold in the women's 100 metres. Just two years previously Doctors nearly had to amputate her feet as a result of radiation treatment for Graves' disease. She would take gold in the same event four years later.

Sergey Bubka (Ukraine) had dominated the pole vault for more than a decade and was expected to win gold comfortably. He failed to record a single clearance despite being the world record holder. (Bubka had previously found a loophole in the way the pole vault was officiated. As part of his appearance fees, he was promised extra money if he broke the world record. Realising that if he moved the bar up by increments of five centimetres (standard procedure) or more he would be doing himself out of valuable bonuses, he upped the bar by one centimetre at a time, thus guaranteeing himself huge payouts after every meeting!)

"Watch the time − it gives you an indication
of how fast they're running"
Ron Pickering

ATLANTA, 1996

The Atlanta Games were poorly administered. The transport system could not cope with the numbers of spectators and athletes, bus drivers were not properly trained and delivered athletes to the wrong events, and the computerised scoring system failed.

Boxing icon Muhammad Ali, shuffling from the effects of Parkinson's disease, lit the Olympic flame in a moment of high emotion.

Veteran sprinter and long-jumper Carl Lewis (USA) won his ninth and last gold medal. Michael Johnson (USA) shattered the world record in the 200 metres sprint with a time of 19.32 seconds. Despite his unorthodox upright style, golden spikes and graceful action, the record is predicted to last for at least another ten years. He completed an outstanding Games with gold in the 400 metres. France's Marie-Jose Perec would match him in the women's equivalent.

ALL-TIME LEADING MEDAL WINNERS BY COUNTRY

COUNTRY	GOLD	SILVER	BRONZE	TOTAL
USA	942	737	643	2322
Russia/USSR	507	425	418	1350
Germany	401	424	453	1278
Great Britain	198	251	249	698
France	210	211	243	664
Italy	199	165	179	543

"Sure there have been injuries and even some deaths in boxing,
but none of them really that serious"
Alan Minter

SYDNEY, 2000

Home favourite Kathy Freeman stormed home to win the 400 metres in Sydney. She had lit the Olympic flame at the opening ceremony. Afghanistan was the only nation to be excluded from the Games.

17 year-old Ian Thorpe (Australia) smashed world and Olympic records in the pool winning three gold and two silver medals in the freestyle sprints.

Michael Johnson (USA) successfully defended his 400 metre crown, but the star of the track was Marion Jones (USA). She won three gold medals (100 metres, 200 metres, 4x400 metre relay) and two bronze (long jump and 4x100 metre relay) to become the first woman to win five track and field medals at a single Games. She would later become involved in the Bay Area Laboratory (BALCO) drugs scandal.

"The swimmers are swimming out of their socks"
Sharron Davies

"Lasse Viren ran a champion's race and came in fifth"
David Coleman

"What a man, what a lift, what a jerk"
Jimmy McGee at the Olympic Weightlifting final

"A brain scan has revealed that Andrew Caddick is not suffering from a stress fracture of the shin"
Jo Sheldon

"If history repeats itself, I should think we can expect the same thing again"
NBC softball announcer

"He dribbles a lot, and the opposition doesn't like it. In fact, you can see it all over their faces"
NBC basketball commentator

"Isn't that nice, the wife of the IOC president is hugging the cox of the British crew"
Harry Carpenter

"One of the reasons Andy is playing so well is that before the final round his wife takes out his balls and kisses them"
NBC tennis announcer

"In terms of the Richter scale, this defeat was a force eight gale"
John Lyall

"There's going to be a real ding-dong when the bell goes"
David Coleman

Denise Lewis (GB) became Olympic heptathlon champion with 6584 points, while team mate Jonathan Edwards claimed the triple jump crown. He'd narrowly missed out in Atlanta despite being the world record holder.

Though the number of Olympic sports remains fairly constant (26-30), the number of events varies dramatically. In Sydney there were 165 events for men and 135 for women, with 12 mixed (equestrian). Women were excluded from boxing (this may change soon) and baseball, while men were excluded from synchronised swimming, softball and rhythmic gymnastics.

"He's even smaller in real life than he is on the track"
David Coleman

ATHENS, 2004

The city had been awarded the Games in 1997 but by 2000 Juan Antonio Samaranch had become so worried at the lack of building progress that he suggested other cities were put on standby. Though the fears over whether the facilities would be ready on time were justified, the Greeks surpassed themselves and the Games were an enormous success. The Olympic flame travelled to every continent on its way to Greece.

The Games were not without controversy, however. Greek athletes Kostas Kenderis, the Olympic 200 metre champion from Sydney, and Katerina Thanou, the 100 metre silver medallist, missed a random drugs test claiming they'd been injured in a motorcycle crash. Kenderis had been handed the honour of lighting the Olympic flame but was forced, or pushed, to pull out. Controversy still surrounds the incident and neither athlete has come up with a satisfactory explanation for the events.

Women competed at Olympia for the first time (shot put).

British sailor Ben Ainslie repeated his gold medal winning performance from Sydney (Laser class) by taking the Finn class honours. His team mate Shirley Robertson made history by becoming the first British woman to win successive Olympic gold medals when she took the Yngling class gold in Athens (with Sarah Ayton and Sarah Webb) to add to her Europe class dinghy gold from Sydney.

Britain's Kelly Holmes completed a historic double by winning the 800- and 1500 metres. The British men's sprint relay team beat the Americans in the closest finish of the Games.

Canoeist Birgit Fischer (Germany) became only the second person to win gold medals at six Olympics (1980, 1988-2004). She would have competed in seven Games were it not for the East German Los Angeles boycott.

Matthew Pinsent (GB) took his fourth consecutive rowing gold medal. He decided to retire shortly afterwards.

Overwhelming favourite (and world record holder) for the women's marathon, Paula Radcliffe (GB) pulled out with less then five miles to go. The extreme heat and steep hills on the course added to the lingering effects of stomach bug to shatter her dream.

IOC President Jacques Rogge announced that a record 24 athletes had tested positive for banned substances (including 12 weightlifters), seven of whom were stripped of their medals. This was an increase of 11 from Sydney, and was, Rogge claimed, proof that they were winning the battle against the cheats. The International Weightlifting Federation was so worried that its poor image would force the IOC to drop it from the Olympics that it set up its own testing program.

American Michael Phelps was the star in the pool. He collected six gold-, and two bronze medals, improving his own world records in the process. He became only the second man to win eight medals at a single Olympics, the other being Russian gymnast Aleksandr Dityatin (1980).

BIZARRE OLYMPIC MOMENTS

Athens 1896:
John Boland (GB), a wealthy tourist, signed up for the
tennis at the last minute and won gold in both the singles
and doubles!

Paris 1900:
The hurdles were made from broken telegraph poles
and the fencing area was in (appropriately) the
World's Fair cutlery centre!

Live pigeons were used in the shooting competition!
(59 didn't survive).

An unknown eight-year-old French boy became the
youngest ever Olympic competitor when he stood in
as a cox in the pairs rowing.

Stan Rowley won three bronze track medals for Australia
and then defected to the British team for the 5000 metres
cross-country where he won gold!

Hungarian Rudolf Bauer was awarded the discus gold
on the strength of three throws that all landed in the crowd!

St. Louis 1904:
George Eyser (USA) won two gymnastics golds –
and six medals overall – even though he was competing
with a wooden leg! He'd lost it having been hit by a train.

The organisers built a steeplechase course consisting of
a variety of objects such as empty beer barrels.

Stockholm 1912:

One of the Greco-Roman wrestling bouts lasted eleven hours and forty minutes! Martin Klein eventually won this semi-final but he was too exhausted to contest the gold medal and it went to Sweden's Claes Johanson by default.

Ralph Craig (USA) won the 100-, and 200 metres, the former after seven false starts, one of which saw him complete the entire distance before being called back.

American Platt Adams won the standing high jump with as leap of 1.63 metres! It was the last time the event was held.

Antwerp 1920:

Grace Kelly's father, John, a bricklayer, won a pair of rowing gold medals.

Paris 1924:

Marathon runners were waited on by servants offering wine and other refreshments!

American Robert LeGendre broke the world long jump record with a leap of 25 feet four inches. Sadly for him the jump was part of the pentathlon and he couldn't replicate the feat in the long jump competition proper and only managed a bronze!

Chamonix 1924:

Anders Haugen (USA) thought he'd placed third in the ski jump but a scoring error denied him a well-deserved bronze. He was finally presented with his medal in 1974. He was 83 years old!

Los Angeles 1932:

Poland's Stanislawa Walasiewicz won the women's 100 metres, becoming the first person to run under 12 seconds.

She was killed in a bungled robbery attempt in 1980 and the autopsy revealed 'her' to be male.

London 1948:
One of the Pakistani swimmers removed his dressing gown before the 100 metres backstroke to find he'd forgotten to wear his trunks! He immediately jumped into the pool to preserve his modesty but was disqualified.

Hungarian army sergeant Karoly Takacs was an unlikely star with a rapid-fire pistol. His right hand had been severed by a grenade blast before the war but he taught himself to shoot with his left and took the gold medal!

Melbourne 1956:
225 people collapsed with heat exhaustion during the opening ceremony.

Tokyo 1964:
The IOC awarded a special Fair Play prize to Swedish yachtsmen Lars Kall and Stig Lennart who rescued two sailors whose boat had sunk and thus missed out on a certain medal! A similar situation would arise 24 years later in Seoul, South Korea. Canadian Lawrence Lemieux was in second place in the Finn class event when he stopped to rescue a drowning Singaporean yachtsman. Lemieux finished in 21st place but was rewarded for his bravery and sacrifice.

Mexico City 1968:
Sweden's Hans-Gunnar Liljenwall became the first athlete to be disqualified for failing a drugs' test. Apparently nervous about the shooting section of the modern pentathlon, he quaffed a few beers and was over the alcohol limit!

Grenoble 1968:

Three East German lugers were disqualified for heating their runners.

Montreal 1976:

Gymnast Shun Fujimoto (Japan) broke his kneecap during the floor exercises. For his country to secure the team gold medal he was required to perform on the rings the next day, and did so without painkillers, sticking the landing and holding the pose for the judges before collapsing in agony.

Boris Onischenko (USSR) was disqualified from the modern pentathlon for cheating. He'd rigged a switch inside his fencing glove so that the scoring light would register false "hits" in his favour!

Toronto Paralympics 1976:

The outstanding athlete was Canadian Arnie Boldt who won the single-leg amputee high jump with an incredible 1.86 metres!

Los Angeles 1984:

Virtually unbeatable over the 400 metre hurdles, Edwin Moses (USA) won his second Olympic title, the first having been in Montreal eight years previously. In between he won a record 122 consecutive races!

Seoul 1988:

Diver Greg Louganis (USA) cracked his head on the diving board attempting a reverse 2 and a half somersault with pike. Though the injury dented his pride more than his head, Louganis successfully defended his springboard title.

Calgary 1988:
The bobsled event will be remembered for the Jamaican entry
crashing on the final turn and inspiring the film *Cool
Runnings* starring John Candy.

Atlanta 1996:
In a moment of high drama, Kerri Strug (USA) hobbled up
to the vault on a badly injured ankle to enable her gymnastics
team to win gold.

Sydney 2000:
Eric 'the Eel' Mossambani (Equatorial Guinea) became
an unlikely star in the pool. His time of 112.72 seconds in
the 100 metre freestyle was not even half as quick
as winner Pieter van den Hoogenband's (Netherlands)
gold medal time!

Marla Runyan (USA) became the first person to
compete at both the Olympics and the Paralympics.
Declared legally blind, she finished eighth in the women's
1500 metres in Sydney having collected six Paralympic
medals in 1992 and 1996.

Athens 2004:
In the men's marathon a spectator (Cornelius Horan)
ran onto the course with five kilometres to go and
pushed Brazilian leader Vanderlei de Lima to the sidelines.
He failed to recover his composure and finished third.
Jacques Rogge presented de Lima with the Pierre de
Coubertin medal for demonstrating exceptional fair play
and the Olympic spirit.

The gymnastics program was blighted by accusations of
poor judging. American Paul Hamm was awarded the
individual all-round gold after an error dropped Korean
Yang Tae-Young to bronze. Hamm was urged to return
his medal in the spirit of sportsmanship! (He didn't).

THE OLYMPIC HYMN

Immortal spirit of antiquity,
Father of the true, beautiful and good,
Descend, appear, shed over us thy light,
Upon this ground and under this sky,
Which has first witnessed thy un-perishable fame.
Give life and animation to those noble Games!
Throw wreaths of fadeless flowers to the victors,
In the race and in strife!
Create in our breasts hearts of steel!
Shine in a roseate hue and form a vast temple,
To which all nations throng to adore thee,
Oh immortal spirit of antiquity.

THE WINTER GAMES

The winter Olympics can be traced back to the London summer Games of 1908. Organisers introduced figure skating, the men's event being won by Ulrich Salchow (Sweden), who gave his name to the backwards jump with one revolution, while Madge Syers (GB) won the women's event.

Germany planned to debut a "Skiing Olympia" featuring Nordic events in the Black Forest at the 1916 summer Games but the event was cancelled due to the outbreak of war in 1914.

CHAMONIX, 1924

In 1920 figure skating and ice hockey were added to the summer program in Antwerp. Then, despite objections from de Coubertin, and the Scandinavian nations, who held their own skiing championships every 4-5 years anyway, the IOC sanctioned an international winter sports week to be held in Chamonix, France. The event included skiing, figure skating, ice hockey and bobsled and was so successful that it was hailed as the first winter Olympics.

The first gold medal was awarded to American speed skater Charles Jewtraw. He won the 500 metres.

Canada scored 104 goals and conceded just two in their first four ice hockey matches. They beat the USA 6-1 in the final.

WINTER OLYMPICS

Year	Venue	Nations	Sports
1924	Chamonix (France)	16	5
1928	St. Moritz (Switzerland)	25	6
1932	Lake Placid (USA)	17	5
1936	Garmisch (Germany)	28	6
1940	Not held		
1944	Not held		
1948	St. Moritz (Switzerland)	28	7
1952	Oslo (Norway)	30	6
1956	Cortina d'Ampezzo (Italy)	32	6
1960	Squaw Valley (USA)	30	6
1964	Innsbruck (Austria)	36	8
1968	Grenoble (France)	37	8
1972	Sapporo (Japan)	35	8
1976	Innsbruck (Austria)	37	8
1980	Lake Placid (USA)	37	8
1984	Sarajevo (Yugoslavia)	49	8
1988	Calgary (Canada)	57	8
1992	Albertville (France)	65	9
1994	Lillehammer (Norway)	67	9
1998	Nagano (Japan)	72	11
2002	Salt Lake City (USA)	78	12
2006	Turin (Italy)		
2010	Vancouver (Canada)		
2014			

Events	Athletes	Medals
14	294	Norway (17)
16	464	Norway (15)
14	252	USA (12)
16	646	Norway (15)
22	706	Nor/Swe (10)
22	694	Norway (16)
24	821	USSR (16)
27	665	USSR (21)
34	1091	USSR (25)
35	1158	Norway (14)
35	1006	USSR (16)
37	1123	USSR (27)
37	1100	USSR/E. Ger
39	1272	E. Ger (24)
46	1750	USSR (29)
57	2174	Germany (26)
61	1737	Norway (26)
68	2177	Germany (29)
78	2399	Germany (35)

"The French are not normally a Nordic skiing nation"
Ron Pickering

ST. MORITZ, 1928

The first Games to be held in a different nation to the summer event, the 1928 winter Olympics in St. Moritz was plagued by warm weather. The 10,000 metres speed skating had to be cancelled while the bobsled and cross-country runs were severely limited.

Sonja Henie (Norway) won the first of her three Olympic golds aged just 15.

"You can observe a lot just by watching"
Yogi Berra

The Games were held every four years until 1992. A two year gap took the winter Games out of step with the summer Olympics, but from 1994 they were again held every four years.

II. OLYMPISCHE
WINTERSPIELE
St. Moritz 11.-19. Febr. 1928

LAKE PLACID, 1932

In 1932 the Games followed the summer Olympics to America. Irving Jaffee was winning the 10,000 metres speed skating in St. Moritz when the track melted and he was denied his medal. At Lake Placid he won the 5,000- and 10,000 metres while local hero Jack Shea won the shorter sprints.

Billy Fiske (USA) steered the four-man bob to victory, adding to the gold he won four years earlier in the five-man event when aged just sixteen. In the team was Eddie Eagan, the Olympic light heavyweight boxing champion from the Antwerp Games. He became the first, and so far only, athlete to win both summer and winter Olympic gold medals.

Only three other athletes have won medals of any colour in both Games: Jacob Tullin Thams (Norway) took the ski jumping gold in 1924 and the eight-metre yachting silver in 1936. Christa Luding-Rothenburger (Germany) took four speed skating medals (1984-1992), two of them gold, and the match sprint cycling silver in 1988. She remains the only athlete to win winter and summer Olympic medals in the same year. Clara Hughes (Canada) won two cycling bronze medals in 1996 and a speed skating bronze in 2002.

> *"I never said most of the things I said"*
> Yogi Berra

GARMISCH-PARTENKIRCHEN, 1936

The fourth winter Games were shared between the neighbouring villages of Garmisch and Partenkirchen in Germany's Bavarian Alps. Alpine skiing was included.

Norwegian speed skater Ivar Ballangrud won three individual

gold medals. His team-mate Sonja Henie won her third straight gold, then, a week later, her 10th world championship.

Britain invited 11 Canadians with British roots to compete on their behalf in the ice hockey. They halted Canada's winning streak at 20 matches and took the gold medal.

Rudi Ball, the Jewish star of the German team was coaxed out of exile by Adolf Hitler as a token gesture to pacify the IOC. They strongly disapproved of the Nazis' anti-Semitic stance and wanted more than a single Jew competing. Their complaints fell on deaf ears.

500,000 people watched the last day's action.

"Baseball is ninety percent mental, the other half is physical"
Yogi Berra

ST. MORITZ, 1948

Both the winter Games at Sapporo and Cortina were cancelled due to the Second World War. The neutral Swiss resort of St. Moritz was chosen for the first Games after hostilities had ceased.

Canada were back to their winning ways on the ice hockey rink. Though their win/loss ratio was the same as Czechoslovakia (7-0-1), they took gold by virtue of their better goal differential (64-62). One of the Czech players, Jaroslav Drobny, went on to have a successful tennis career, winning Wimbledon in 1954.

"And there are four Brazilians on the beach-volleyball court,
none of them from South America"
A Eurosport commentator anticipates
a great women's final

OSLO, 1952

Dick Button continued where he'd left off in Switzerland by winning the figure skating gold. He turned professional shortly afterwards. The male star of the Games was the Norwegian, Hjalmar Andersen, a truck driver, who won three speed skating gold medals and set two Olympic records.

The Canadians took their seventh gold from eight attempts in the ice hockey by beating the US in the final. They wouldn't win another for fifty years.

"Where were the Germans? And, frankly, who cares?"
Barry Davies enjoys Britain's
1988 hockey gold medal

CORTINA, 1956

A shortage of snow hampered the event but some remarkable performances were achieved, most notably by the Austrian skier Toni Sailer. Tying string around the ankles of his ski pants to stop them flapping, he won the downhill, slalom and giant slalom for a clean sweep of the skiing medals

The Soviet Union had emerged from its self imposed exile to take overall second place in the medals' table at the summer Games in Helsinki four years earlier. In Cortina they finished top of the winter table and dethroned the previously unbeatable Canadians in the ice hockey final. Four of their golds came in the speed skating with Yevgeny Grishin taking the 500- and 1500 metre titles

"We're 2-0 up here, boys. And we're winning"
Dave Archer

SQUAW VALLEY, 1960

Squaw Valley was a tiny Californian ski resort near Lake Tahoe. It had no bobsled run and, until two days before the opening ceremony, no snow.

The ice hockey tournament was supposed to be a two horse race between the Russians and Canadians, but the American team surprised them both, beating their northerly neighbours 2-1 and the USSR 3-2. Then they beat the Czechs 9-4 in the final.

Yevgeny Grishin (USSR) starred again, repeating his 500- and 1500 metre wins on the speed skating track. He actually tied the 1500 metres at both Games, first with Yuri Mikhailov (USSR) and then with Norwegian Roald Aas.

Women speed skaters were allowed to compete for the first time, with Russia's Lydia Skoblikova taking two golds. She would take four more at Innsbruck four years later, the first time any athlete had won four golds at a single Games.

"It gets late early out there"
Yogi Berra

INNSBRUCK, 1964

The lead up to the ninth winter Games in Innsbruck in the Tyrolean Alps was marred by tragedy. In 1961 eighteen members of the US figure skating team – including their top female skater Laurence Owen – had been killed in a plane crash in Belgium. Then, in the week before the Games themselves, Ross Milne, a young Australian skier and Kazimierz Kay-Skyszpeski, a British luger, were killed in practice runs. Warm weather was also a problem. The Austrian army had to import over 50,000 cubic metres of snow to make up for the warm temperatures lower down in the village.

Sisters Christine and Marielle Goitschel (France) each took a skiing gold and silver.

> *"It's 0-0 here, with England very much on level terms"*
> Nigel Starmer-Smith

GRENOBLE, 1968

The Games in France were a great success, particularly for the host nation, thanks largely to 24-year-old skiing sensation Jean-Claude Killy. He became the first male athlete to complete the clean sweep of the skiing medals since Toni Sailer (Austria) in 1956. He was only awarded the gold in the slalom, however, after the original 'winner', Karl Schranz (Austria), was found to have missed two gates. The unlucky Austrian retired after the 1972 Games (having been barred from competition – see money matters) and never won Olympic gold. In a statement released after the event he said that "the Olympics should be a competition of skill, strength and speed – and no more."

SAPPORO, 1972

Magnar Solberg (Norway) became the oldest male champion when he won the 20 kilometre biathlon title (35 years and 4 days). Christina Baas-Kaiser won the 3000 metre speed skating gold at 33 years and 268 days to become the oldest female winner.

> *"He's accelerating all the time. The last lap was run in 64 seconds, the one before in 62"*
> David Coleman

INNSBRUCK, 1976

The Games were originally awarded to Denver, but Colorado residents voted against helping to finance the event and the city was forced to withdraw. The IOC decided Innsbruck should host the Games despite having just done so (1964).

John Curry (GB) took gold in the figure skating to add to his British, European and World titles for a unique 'Grand Slam'. Dorothy Hamill won the women's event.

Hans van Helden (Netherlands) was the only man to win three medals. Sadly for him, they were all bronze (speed skating)!

"Wherever I go people are waving at me.
Maybe if I do a good job they'll start to use all their fingers"
Frank King,
Winter Olympic Games organising committee chairman

LAKE PLACID, 1980

The Games will be remembered for some truly outstanding performances. In a feat never managed before or since, Eric Heiden, a young American speed skater won gold in all five race disciplines (500-, 1000-, 1500-, 5000- and 10,000 metres). His tally of individual golds at a single Olympics beats the efforts of Mark Spitz, three of whose swimming medals came in relay events. On the morning of the 10,000 metres Heiden overslept and had to dash seven miles down to the rink having only eaten a slice of bread for breakfast.

Alpine skiing legend Ingemar Stenmark (Sweden) won his only two Olympic gold medals in Lake Placid. Having won the slalom and giant slalom, he went on to take 86 World Cup victories before retiring in 1989.

Robin Cousins (GB) took over from John Curry by winning the figure skating gold.

The American ice hockey team had been thrashed by the Russians in an exhibition match a week before the Games. They went into the Olympics knowing they would have to turn round a 10-3 score-line to upset the champions. Captain Mike Eruzione scored the winner midway through the third period. Goalie Jim Craig pulled off 39 saves and they held on to win 4-3. They comfortably beat Finland in the final.

SARAJEVO, 1984

By the time the Games returned to Europe in 1984, the East German team had become the continent's dominant force. Karin Enke was their star in Sarajevo, winning two gold medals and two silvers in the women's speed skating. The only woman to win three individual titles was Finland's cross-country skier Marja-Liisa Hamalainen.

The US team shone in the alpine disciplines for the first time. Brothers Phil and Steve Mahre finished 1-2 in the slalom while compatriot Bill Johnson took the downhill.

The stand-out performance of the winter Games came from British ice dancers Jayne Torvill and Christopher Dean. They'd come fifth in Lake Placid but had perfected their routine by 1984. Dancing to Ravel's Bolero on Valentine's Day, they scored the maximum six points from all the judges to secure a place in Olympic history. Many thought that their routine in Lillehammer ten years later was good enough for gold, but the judges controversially ruled that they had made an illegal manoeuvre and they only managed bronze.

CALGARY, 1988

Matti Nykanen (Finland) became the first ski jumper to win three gold medals. He claimed first position in the 70- and 90 metre hills and the team jumping.

Britain sent plasterer Eddie 'the Eagle' Edwards to compete in the ski jumping. Despite having no proper training (he hand-built a metal contraption in his back yard to help his technique on take-off), he showed the peculiarly English trait of having a go against insurmountable odds. However, the event is highly dangerous and he was, in fact, risking his life. Despite crashing on many jumps, he managed to come 58th and last on the 70 metre hill and 55th and last on the 90 metre! He was mobbed on his return to London and remains something of a celebrity today.

ALBERTVILLE, 1992

Two athletes won five medals. Elena Valbe (Russia) took a gold and four bronzes, while team mate Lyubov Egorova claimed three golds and two silvers in the cross-country skiing. Egorova and Lydia Skoblikova (Russia) would become the most success-ful female Olympians of all time with six gold medals. Compatriot Raisa Smetanina, the only woman to medal in five consecu-tive Games (1976-1992), won more medals overall but only four were golds.

Toni Nieminen (Finland) won the 90 metre hill ski jump to become the youngest ever winter Olympic champion (16 years 261 days).

LILLEHAMMER, 1994

The Lillehammer Games were held just two years after Albertville so they would no longer coincide with the summer Olympics.

One event in particular will be remembered above all others: the women's figure skating. Just before the US figure skating championships, favourite Nancy Kerrigan was attacked by a man who tried to break her legs. It emerged that rival Tonya Harding, had ordered the attack to give her a better chance of winning the Olympics. The plot failed and Kerrigan went on to take the silver medal. Harding, who'd threatened an expensive lawsuit if she wasn't allowed to compete, finished eighth, but her career was in tatters. The final was the sixth highest rated program in US television history.

Johann Koss (Norway) won three gold medals with three world records in the speed skating (1500-, 5000- and 10,000 metres).

NAGANO, 1998

The weather was totally unpredictable in Nagano—there was even an earthquake! With organisers struggling to have all the events completed on time, they were forced to hold the men's super giant slalom, the women's downhill and the women's combined downhill on a single day.

Curling and snowboarding debuted.

Hermann 'the Herminator' Maier (Austria), one of the most
powerful skiers of all time, survived a horrifying crash during
the men's downhill. He recovered to win two gold medals over
the next week.

Tara Lipinski (USA) claimed gold in the figure skating aged
just 15 years and 256 days to become the youngest female
champion.

Bjorn Dahlie (Norway) starred again. He won four medals in
the cross-country skiing to take his tally to twelve Olympic
medals, eight of them gold. But it was the women who stole the
show. Larissa Lazutina (Russia) won five medals (three gold)
also in the cross-country. She would test positive for darbepo-
etin four years later and would be stripped of her medals from
Salt Lake City, though not the five she won in Nagano.

The Czech Republic were surprise winners of the coveted ice
hockey title, beating Russia 1-0 in the final. The US team
consisted solely of professionals and had been predicted to win

CURRENT TABLE OF WINTER SPORTS

Alpine	Ice Hockey
Skiing	Luge
Biathlon	Nordic Skiing
Bobsled	Ski Jumping
Curling	Snowboarding
Figure Skating	Speed Skating
Freestyle Skiing	

comfortably but they blew their chances and then wrecked their changing rooms.

Hosts Japan scored five golds out of a total of ten medals, thanks largely to the efforts of ski jumpers Kazuyoshi Funaki (two golds) and Masahiko Harada, and speed skater Hiroyasu Shimizu.

SALT LAKE CITY, 2002

The Games in Salt Lake City would prove to be the most controversial yet. It emerged that several IOC members received gifts in exchange for casting their votes in favour of the host city. At least four members resigned, as did most of the city's committee officials. Then Canadian figure skating pair Jamie Sale and David Pelletier were awarded equal first place after one of the judges admitted to being pressurized into awarding the Russian pair (Elena Berezhnaya and Anton Sikharulidze) higher marks. The IOC promised to review the scoring system before the next Olympics.

Vonetta Flowers (USA) became the first black athlete to win winter gold (Bobsledding).

The event was also marred by a number of high-profile doping scandals. Britain's Alain Baxter lost his bronze slalom medal despite proving the banned substance was in a Vicks inhaler.

Steven Bradbury (Australia) won gold in the short track speed skating, the first for any country in the southern hemisphere.

Multiple crashes in the semi-final and final certainly helped.

Canada's men and women beat the USA into silver in both the ice hockey competitions. For the Canadian men it had been fifty years to the day since they last took gold in the event.

Rhona Martin (GB) skippered the British women to a 4-3 curling victory over Switzerland and the gold medal. The country's first winter Olympic gold for 18 years was clinched with the last stone of the final end.

German luger Georg Hackl became the first Olympian to win five consecutive gold medals in the same individual event (1988-2002). Only one other man had medalled in five winter Olympics – Harri Kirvesniemi (Finland, 1980-1998).

"He just can't believe what's not happening to him"
David Coleman

THE PARALYMPIC GAMES

In the same year that London held the first Olympics after the Second World War (1948), Sir Ludwig Guttmann proposed and held a sports competition involving war veterans with spinal cord injuries in Stoke Mandeville, England. The idea took off and athletes from the Netherlands joined the event at the same venue four years later.

When organisers of the Rome summer Olympics (1960) suggested a parallel competition with Olympic style sports for those with a disability, the Paralympic movement came of age. In fact the prefix 'para' comes from the Greek meaning 'beside' or 'alongside' and does not derive directly from paralysis or paraplegia as is commonly believed. They are in every sense the "Parallel Games".

In September 1989 a new governing body – the International Paralympic Committee (IPC) – was established. It replaced the International Coordinating Committee (ICC) that had managed the movement since 1982. The three 'comma' shapes called *"Tae-Geuks"* found on the Paralympic flag represent the "Mind, Body and Spirit". They also symbolise the new vision of the International Paralympic Committee: "To enable Paralympic athletes to achieve sporting excellence and to inspire and excite the world." Four words sum up the spirit and vision of Paralympians: pursuit, strength, inspiration and celebration. "Spirit in Motion" is their motto.

PARALYMPIC SUMMER GAMES

Year	Venue	Nations	Sports
1960	Rome (Italy)	23	8
1964	Tokyo (Japan)	21	9
1968	Tel Aviv (Israel)	29	9
1972	Heidelberg (Germany)	41	10
1976	Toronto (Canada)	40	11
1980	Arnhem (Netherlands)	42	12
1984	Stoke Mandeville (GB) & New York (USA)	45	14
1988	Seoul (South Korea)	61	16
1992	Barcelona (Spain)	82	15
1996	Atlanta (USA)	103	20
2000	Sydney (Australia)	122	18
2004	Athens (Greece)	140	19
2008	Beijing (China)		
2012	London (Great Britain)		

By 1976 other disability groups had been added to the program. In fact, changes are regularly made to the classification system so that athletes of similar abilities can compete against one another. Teams gathered at an event in Toronto coinciding with the summer Olympics in Montreal. With the event a huge success, it was decided to amalgamate all other groups so that a single Paralympic event could be held every four years. That same year, the first winter Paralympic Games were held in Sweden.

Today, athletes from six well defined disability groups may compete. They are: amputees, cerebral palsy, les autres (comprises a variety of conditions such as dwarfism or multiple sclerosis), intellectually impaired, visually impaired and wheelchair athletes.

Events	Athletes	Medals
57	400	USA (43)
144	375	USA(122)
181	750	USA (99)
190	1004	Germany (67)
527	1657	USA (155)
1001	1973	USA (174)
559	2900	USA (276)
156	3053	USA (268)
487	3020	USA (175)
501	3195	USA (157)
550	3824	Australia (149)
571	3969	China (141)

Since Seoul 1988 the Paralympic Games have been held at the same city as the summer Olympics. The same goes for the winter Games since Albertville (1992).

ROME, 1960

Sir Ludwig Guttman's dream was realised when the 9th Annual International Stoke Mandeville Games came to Rome. (The IOC would only recognise them as the first official Paralympic Games in 1984). There were a few problems hosting the event immediately after the summer Olympics. The athletes' village was not wheelchair-friendly and transporting competitors to the athletics and basketball arenas proved time consuming. 5000 spectators watched the opening ceremony in the Acqua Acetosa stadium six days after the summer Olympic closing ceremony.

As most of the competitors had spinal cord injuries, the list of sports was adapted to include snooker, precision javelin and dart archery.

Dick Thompson (GB) was the star on the track with gold medals in the club throw (34.85 metres), class A and B javelin (19.33 metres), precision javelin (70 points) and a bronze in the shot put (6.42 metres). Local hero Franco Rossi fenced beautifully and the all-conquering Americans took gold in the basketball.

"The opening ceremony was like a rock concert.
The only thing missing was Pink Floyd"
Steve Ovett

TOKYO, 1964

Support for holding the Paralympic Games after the Olympics had risen and the Japanese staged the next event. The opening ceremony was also watched by about 5000 spectators and held at the Oda Field inside the athletes' village. Wheelchair racing debuted and is now considered one of the Paralympic highlights.

Ron Stein (USA) backed up his achievements of four years earlier with gold in the 60 metre wheelchair race, gold in the special pentathlon, and gold in each of the class D club, discus, shot put and javelin. Briton Dick Thompson (class A club- and javelin gold, class A shot put silver, 60 metre wheelchair bronze and class 1 pentathlon bronze) also had a memorable Games.

"There's a great advantage to be able to swim inside the legs
of the man in front of you"
David Wilkie

TEL AVIV, 1968

Though Mexican officials had planned to host the 1968 Paralympic Games, they decided to pull out – citing technical difficulties – some two years before the event was due to be held. Israel stepped in and staged the Games to coincide with its 20th year of independence.

Italian Roberto Marson was the outstanding performer of the Games. He'd won two field event gold medals in 1964 but returned four years later having trained extensively to win swimming and fencing medals as well. He claimed a total of nine gold medals, three in each discipline.

"Here we are in the Holy land of Israel, a Mecca for tourists"
David Vine

HEIDELBERG, 1972

Though the Paralympic committee tried to stage the event in Munich to coincide with the summer Olympics, the city had already agreed to turn the Olympic village into private apartments. The mayor of Heidelberg stepped in to offer his city's assistance and the Games were held at the university's institute for physical training where athletes could refresh themselves in an enormous beer tent!

The US basketball team made up for their loss four years earlier with a 59-58 win over defending champions Israel. The game was watched by more than 4000 spectators.

"Well that's enough about depressing drugs scandals at these Games. I'll try to remain positive for the rest of this discussion"
Leann Paulick

TORONTO, 1976

Television coverage enabled more than 600,000 viewers in southern Ontario alone to tune in. In wheelchair athletics, longer distances (up to 1500 metres) were the main difference.

> *"And now Sepeng takes the lead, absolutely*
> *surrounded by other runners"*
> Martin Gillingham

ARNHEM, 1980

Though Moscow had been approached, the Soviet Sports Ministry declined to host the 1980 Games. Cities from Denmark, South Africa and the Netherlands all offered their support and the bid finally went to Arnhem. South Africa was denied the chance to compete as it still promoted the policy of apartheid. The class system had been revised again and there were over 3000 medals up for grabs.

Trischa Zorn (USA) won seven gold medals in the pool.

Canadian Arnie Boldt took another gold and increased his own world record to 1.96 metres in the single-leg amputee high jump!

> *"Yelena Isinbayeva loves to get hold of a stiff pole –*
> *soft ones are no good to her"*
> Paul Dickenson

> *"Triathlon is an intensely individual sport, and these guys*
> *all compete for each other"*
> Simon Lessing

STOKE MANDEVILLE AND NEW YORK, 1984

In 1977 the IOC announced that the 1984 Paralympic games would be held in Los Angeles, but the voluntary organising committees had no direct contact with the IOC. In 1980 the American National Wheelchair Athletic Association (ANWAA) suggested that it held an event in New York with the three other disability groups – amputees, cerebral palsy athletes and the visually impaired, while those with spinal cord injuries competed in Stoke Mandeville.

Reiner Kuschall (Switzerland) and Bart Dodson (USA) won two gold medals on the track. Canadian Rick Hansen won gold in the 1500 metres and the marathon. He would later wheel his chair around the world on his Man-in-Motion Tour!

The Games were a great success but many felt they were too disjointed. The sports federations governing each disability unified under the name, "The International Coordinating Committee of World Organisations for the Disabled" (ICC), as a direct result.

> *"Currently taking place is the high jump pole vault,*
> *which is part of the decathlon"*
> Dickie Broberg

SEOUL, 1988

A record crowd of 75,000 watched the opening ceremony.

Mustapha Badid (France) won four gold wheelchair racing medals (200 metres, 1500 metres, 5000 metres and marathon) while Connie Hansen (Denmark) took gold in the 400-, 800-, 1500- 5000 metres and marathon. Dennis Oelher (USA) ran the 100 metres with a prosthetic leg in 11.73.seconds.

Trischa Zorn (USA), a visually-impaired swimmer, won 12 gold medals, including ten individual titles and two relays. In so doing, she set nine world records!

"I was wondering when the Marathon would bite back at Paula Radcliffe. It's a cruel distance, it lies in wait for you, and when you least expect it, it suddenly jumps up and bites you in the bum"
Steve Cram

BARCELONA, 1992

Barcelona officials took the controversial step of reducing the number of events so that athletes with slightly different disabilities could compete against one another and would be guaranteed to fill the eight places in each event. The Games were the most successful to date.

Swimmer Trischa Zorn (USA) won another ten gold- and two silver medals. John Morgan and Elizabeth Scott (both USA) also swam impressively, picking up eight and seven golds respectively.

A capacity crowd watched the end of the men's wheelchair marathon. Heinz Frei (Switzerland) beat 196 athletes to place first in 1 hour and 30 minutes, a full half hour quicker than the Olympic runners! Connie Hansen repeated her feat from four years earlier and won the women's event in 1 hour 42 minutes and 48 seconds.

Single-arm amputee Ajibola Adeoye (Nigeria) turned in the performance of the Games. He won the 100 metres in 10.72 seconds, a time that, it has been calculated by scientists, would have been 10.05 seconds if he'd had the benefit of both arms, good enough for fourth in the Olympics.

TABLE OF CURRENT PARALYMPIC SUMMER SPORTS

Archery	Judo	Wheelchair Dance
Athletics	Powerlifting	
Basketball	Sailing	Wheelchair Fencing
Boccia	Shooting	
Bowls Cycling	Swimming	Wheelchair Rugby
Equestrian	Table Tennis	
Football	Volleyball	Wheelchair Tennis
Goalball		

ATLANTA, 1996

The Atlanta Games were the first to attract worldwide corporate sponsorship deals. 56 athletes with intellectual disabilities were allowed to compete. Racquetball, wheelchair rugby and sailing were included as demonstration events.

Louise Sauvage (Australia) won four wheelchair racing gold medals (400-, 800-, 1500- and 5000 metres).

57,640 spectators packed the grandstands for the closing ceremony.

> *"Bennett is a great fan of giving it to himself,*
> *and here he is − giving it to himself"*
> Simon Lessing

"This man was not on anyone's lips yesterday, yet here he is —
an Olympic bronze medallist"
Danie Malan

OOOO

SYDNEY, 2000

Olympic and Paralympic athletes shared the same accommodation, medical care, catering, sports facilities and transport links,
which blended seamlessly from one event to the next. As a
result the event was hailed as the best yet.

Swimmer Jason Wening (USA), a double amputee, won his
third consecutive 400 metre freestyle gold medal, claiming a
world record in the process. He had not been beaten in his class
since 1991!

Britain's extraordinary wheelchair athlete Tanni Grey-
Thompson won four gold medals (100-, 200-, 400- and 800
metres). She had won silvers in the 100-, 200- and 400 metres
in Atlanta as well as a gold in the 800 metres. In Barcelona she'd
won four golds and a silver, and in Seoul she claimed a solitary
bronze. She would go on to take another two golds in Athens.
Her overall Paralympic tally amounted to 11 class golds from 16
medals at five Games. She has not denied rumours that she may
yet compete in Beijing!

The official website registered more than 300 million hits
during the event.

"Now let's go over and see what happened in the gold medal hockey
match, which was won by Australia against Holland earlier today"
Leann Paulick

ATHENS, 2004

Spectator numbers increased from just 5000 in Rome in 1960 to 80,000 in 1984. By Sydney 2000 a record 1.2 million tickets had been sold, though this dropped to 800,000 for Athens. There were more than 600 drug tests performed on Paralympians, with seven positive results.

Swimmers Jim Anderson and David Roberts (both GB) finished with four gold medals apiece.

"The last time the USA was defeated in the 4x400 metres relay was back in 1980 when they didn't compete"
Leann Paulick

"Pole vaulter Guiseppe Gibilisco has a great passion for riding motorcycles, but he's actually afraid to ride them for fear of damaging his legs, so you'll never actually see him on one"
Martin Gillingham

PARALYMPIC WINTER GAMES

Although some organised ski racing for those with disabilities had been around since about 1950, it was not until 1976 that an event was put together with the sole aim of allowing athletes to compete against one another equally, and for medals. The first world championships had been held in Grand Bornand (France) two years earlier but the idea really took off with the announcement that the Paralympics would get a winter event.

ORNSKOLDSVIK, 1976

Only alpine and cross-country skiing medals were contested by amputee and visually impaired athletes, while sledge racing was a demonstration event.

Swiss giant slalom legend Elisabeth Osterwalder claimed gold in the women's LW3 event. The Swiss team would go on to take nine gold out of their 11 medals.

GEILO, 1980

All classes of athletes with locomotor disabilities were declared eligible to compete.

Norwegian Hans Anton Aalien took gold in the men's B1 long distance ski, while the Swedish women won gold in the 4x5 kilometre relay by eight minutes.

There was a downhill sledge racing demonstration event with athletes reaching speeds of over 100 kilometres per hour (60mph).

INNSBRUCK, 1984

30 male three track skiers (skiing on one leg using two crutches with skis attached) took part in a giant slalom exhibition event at the Sarajevo winter Olympics.

Veronica Preining (Austria) won the B1 ladies' downhill.

"That's the fastest time ever run – but it's not quite as fast as the world record"
David Coleman

INNSBRUCK, 1988

Though the Games were to have been held immediately after the winter Olympics in Calgary, recruiting and financial problems forced the organisers to choose a tried and tested venue and the Games returned to Innsbruck. The USSR sent a team to the Games for the first time. Ice sledge racing and sit-skiing made their debuts.

Biathlon was included for the first time. Per-Erik Larsson (Sweden) won gold in the men's LW2 class scoring the maximum possible shooting points.

ALBERTVILLE/TIGNES, 1992

There were no facilities for ice sports in Albertville so only the alpine and Nordic events were held. There were demonstration events for intellectually disabled athletes in the alpine and cross-country skiing disciplines.

Cato Pedersen (Norway) lit the Paralympic torch and won gold in the super-g (super-giant slalom). He took another gold and a silver in his other alpine disciplines.

The winter Paralympics only started sharing venues with the Olympics after Albertville.

LILLEHAMMER, 1994

Sweden won the ice sledge hockey final – a debut event – by beating Norway 1-0 in a penalty shootout. The home side won gold in the sit-ski relay.

Biathlon's popularity had been growing steadily and 24 teams

PARALYMPIC WINTER GAMES

Year	Venue	Nations	Athletes	Medals
1976	Ornskoldsvik (Sweden)	14	250	Austria (35)
1980	Geilo (Norway)	18	350	Finland (29)
1984	Innsbruck (Austria)	22	350	Austria (82)
1988	Innsbruck (Austria)	22	397	Norway
1992	Albertville/Tignes (France)	24	475	USA (45)
1994	Lillehammer (Norway)	34	500	Norway (64)
1998	Nagano (Japan)	32	571	Norway
2002	Salt Lake City (USA)	35	550	Germany
2006	Turin (Italy)			
2010	Vancouver (Canada)			

sent athletes to compete in this gruelling event. Marjorie van de Bunt (Netherlands) won gold in the amputee division while Anne-Mette Bredahl-Christiansen (Denmark) won the visually impaired gold.

The Games of the VI Paralympiad attracted over a million spectators.

NAGANO, 1998

Athletes with an intellectual disability were permitted to compete in the first winter Paralympics to be held outside Europe. Over ten days of competition, athletes contested 34 events from five sports. These were: alpine skiing, cross-country skiing, biathlon, ice sledge racing and ice sledge hockey. Alpine skiing was further divided into downhill, super giant slalom, giant slalom and slalom.

Blind skiers followed a sighted guide who issued voice commands about which way to turn. Those with limb disabilities used specially adapted equipment, including the single ski, sit-ski or orthopaedic ski.

The Nagano Games showed a clear increase in media interest in disabled sport. More than 150,000 spectators attended the events and the Games' website attracted over 8 million hits.

SALT LAKE CITY, 2002

The Games were an extraordinary success, with more than 250,000 spectators. China, Chile and Greece participated for the first time.

The star of the event was undoubtedly 58-year old Raghnhild Myklebust (Norway). Competing in the sit-skiing, her gold brought her total medal tally to 21 in five Olympiads. Sarah Will (USA) won two golds on the slopes taking her total to 11 overall.

The US beat defending champions Norway in the final of the men's ice sledge hockey. A capacity 10,000 crowd watched the event.

TURIN, 2006

Wheelchair curling will make its debut in Turin.

40 nations have applied to send 580 athletes to Italy.

VANCOUVER, 2010

45 countries will contribute nearly 700 athletes to the X Paralympiad in Canada.

The following sources of information were
particularly helpful when compiling this book.

www.perseus.tufts.edu/Olympics
www.olympic.org/uk
www.about.com
www.britishathletics.info
www.sport.guardian.co.uk
www.gamesinfo.com.au
www.infoplease.com
www.news.bbc.co.uk
www.nationmaster.com
www.factbites.com
www.paralympicgames.torino.2006.org
www.users.skynet.be
www.cbc.ca/olympics
www.paralympic.ca
www.psychedonline.org

The Guinness book of sporting heroes

I would like to thank Ashley Gaunt and Seamus McCann for
their helpful suggestions on what to include, and Derek Benning
for instilling me with a passion for the subject.

When writing a fact filled book of this nature I am invariably
faced with conflicting information from a number of sources.
I have then had to make a judgement on what seemed to me
to be the most accurate version of events. I have undoubtedly
made some errors, for which I apologise, and will gladly correct
them as and when they are made known to me. I would also
like to apologise for the material I have been forced to omit
due to considerations of space. The Olympics is an enormous
subject and simply cannot be crammed into the 20,000 or so
words I had at my disposal.